C.R.A.P

C.R.A.P

Cold. Rolled.
Annealed. Pickled

RAVI KODUKULA

PARTRIDGE

To order additional copies of this book, contact
Partridge India
000 800 10062 62
orders.india@partridgepublishing.com

www.partridgepublishing.com/india

C.R.A.P

Cold... Rolled... Annealed... Pickled

Now that you hold this book in your hand... let me talk to you for a while... not that you are a dimwit... but I am sure you would have figured this out by now...

This book does not have any purpose or meaning... there's already a lot of crap flying around in the publishing world... so, I just thought of adding some more... really...

This book does not come from somebody highly accomplished or acclaimed... in fact this book does not intend to cause that earthshattering shift too – towards any acclamation...

There is no Foreword... Middles... or Epilogue to this book...

There are no endorsements from highly acclaimed litter-ateurs...

This book does not claim to be a bestseller and will never get to be one...

This book does not address a social cause... it does not solve the carbon catastrophe that you see around you...

This is not a self-help book... so... no philosophy... no quantum physics... no next gen robotics in here...

And... this book is definitely not from the wannabe stables of a Booker or a Pulitzer...

This book – at its worst – can go down the bookshelves as the "World According to Me"... with anecdotal references to growing up in middle class urban India in the 70's and the 80's... and carving out a life, meaningful in most ways, in the 90's and beyond... as meaningful as the fast changing environment that I saw in India and the world around ME...

Having grown up and lived in Delhi most of my life... I conveniently say – I am a hardcore Indian in values... and *'Punjabi By Nature'*... I *'Think in Punjabi'* when I am driving... otherwise I just can't drive in this country... even in Mumbai... my home for the last 7 years...

My experiences could be yours... and if I caught you smiling in your sleep as you connected with one of mine... I would feel obliged... but I cannot guarantee that smile in your sleep... as I know many of these experiences of mine... are mine...

I published this book because... simply... I wanted to publish a book in life... and if you accidentally bought it... or you are reading this because somebody gifted this to you... I am happy... as that would mean, at least one more person is reading this – apart from me...

I have bared a good part of my life with you here... if it resonates with you in any way or if you have a story to share... I would love to hear your story...

Thank You... for being a part of my life...

This book is dedicated to – ME

(Honestly, I did not find anybody else worthy of taking this crap...)

But... my anecdotal references take me into the hearts of many people that I have grown up and breathed life with...

Many of who, are quite relaxed when I told them they are going to find their names in here...

Many, who wanted me to change their names to protect their sanity... and my senility...

Many brands and companies that I have worked with... or used... I have cherished each moment of having been associated with them and have all the love for each one of them... despite the fact that some of my employers had sacked me...

Some references are in languages other than English... and I have made an attempt to convert the true essence in English... but they are still best read in the native tongue... that's the beauty in the diversity of languages in India...

Much of what I have written... is all that I scribbled between one meeting at my workplace and the next... in my life as an upcoming corporate fat cat... so, none of them may tie back to each other...

So,... relax... you could start with somewhere in the middle... go right to the end and then come back to the start of this classic script...

Much of what you read here is a conversion of my blogs written across time... over the last many years at www.fursatfriday.com I still write there... every Friday...

Each of the stories that I have shared in this book has a context and a reference to time when the events happened in my life...

While I have tried keeping the context timeless...

A . (full stop) stops time...

A ... (suspension point) is a continuum...

With Malice...

Towards One and All...

And towards None at All...

What's In Here?

1

From the BC... to the Bimmer...

18 years... renewal of vows... same woman... much
cheaper this way...

This is how it all began...

*"Ravi, will you drop her home please? She has been
waiting for a long time for you to get back home, so
that you could drop her. It's quite late. Her parents may
be really worrying."*

My mother's words still ring in my ears...

I didn't smell rat when my mother said this the first time... nor did I have any idea of a conspiracy brewing between two new found friends... one a 45 year old woman who gave birth to me... and another pretty nearly half her age at that time... who would bear my children in the future...

The third woman who completed this equation and who played the perfect panderer for this fast developing subterfuge... the woman behind the strategy... was my younger sister...

When you rode 20 odd kilometres in a dusky, smoggy week day evening through some of the most smoke infested traffic zones of Delhi in the mid-90's and got home late in the evening... well 8pm was late in a January Delhi then (perhaps even today)... you would hope to catch an early dinner and catch up on a book and start snoring after the 5th page...

Trust me... you are pooped...!

Particularly if you were me... who on most weekdays opened the shutters of my employer's Connaught Place office at 7 in the morning... for the record... I did that most part of my 2 year stint in that role of mine... if my attendance records with my employer would not verify this... the round the corner chaat-waala in A Block Connaught Place, would be the most definite witness...

"Not today, Amma. I am really tir..."

I stopped myself mid-sentence... drop her home... drop a girl home... drop THIS girl home...

Fresh out of my sister's room, came out two girls... one whom I had always held in my arms and played with ever since she was born as my sister... and the other... as destiny would decide... would waft into my arms... and my life like a thousand delightful fragrances...

One of the most under-articulated pleasures of growing up in middle class India was the BC... well... the much ubiquitous, motored biped of the 80's and the 90's...

Our very own **Hamara Bajaj... Bajaj Chetak...**

Amazingly so, when you have just promised your mother that you would drop the girl home that she has asked you to... rather ordered...

A half hour ago the BC was the scourge of all maladies that ailed a smoked up and fumed down conurbation like Delhi... and now... it was god sent *'Pushpaka Vimana'* (the mythological flying chariot)...

With Smita on the pillion... the distance of 6 kilometers from my home to hers... which would otherwise border on drudgery... seemed like... the BC just took to its wings... has turned into the **'Flying Chetak'**...

Smita... Smee, as I call her now... came into my life, due an act of a deep seated, meticulously planned conspiracy theory flawlessly played out into action... not a word misplaced in screenplay... not a frame lost in editing...

The BC was but, a prop in the play... it took an instant liking for Smee... and Smee could for once, during those evenings when she would ride the pillion on the BC... could let go of the small little pleasures that the crowded and noisome DTC (Delhi Transport Corporation) would offer...

4 months later... and a few occasions that she was stalled at my home on the same lame, *"Ravi-would-come-soon-enough-and-would-drop-you-home"* pretext... my mother popped the question that I most feared...

"Smita has been coming home quite often now... she is your sister's friend... I quite like her... she is almost a friend to me now... how would you like our home to be a final homecoming for her?"

In that rare nano-moment of particulate suspension... when all matter stood still... when the fission and fusion were momentarily non-complimentary spiritual processes... when the left and the right brains refused to impress upon each other... I did a very quick logicalculation...

I thought of all those women that I had popped the question, "Would you please come home and meet my parents"... and all of who declined, for their bitter distaste for the BC... for a better taste of a Maruti 800 (the sign of having arrived in life in middle class India of those times)...

Smee's final homecoming seemed most logically certain...

While the BC was still around... Smita riding the pillion while we were courting, after our agreement to tie the knot... I did elevate to a Maruti 800...

The BC was good for courting your Fiancee... but never good enough to drive your Wife home...

And what's more... as a scholar devoted to Venusian harmony... and through all the chronicles that are legibly available in true validation of both my mother and wife's self proclaimed camaraderie... I could see quite quickly... that my mother and my wife were really very good friends... till I got married...

Even to date... read however hard I may... peculiar are Venusian ways... my mother and my wife continue to be best of buddies as they are 7 rivers apart...

That fateful wedding day... 18 years ago in November 1997... bliss unfolded in myriad ways... I switched roles – I became a husband... Smee switched homes – became my partner for life...

We had long decided that we would get married every 5 years... try and see if that has to be to the same person... no promises made though...

We end up getting married to each other... it's cheaper this way...

Smee is thrifty... she made me sell off the BC the day before our wedding... *"we don't need 2 vehicles,"* she had said...

I am the squanderer... My Maruti 800 made an American Bank richer through my first loan in life... and many adventures and many more banks later... the BMW made its way into our lives 2 years ago...

Just so that Smee foregoes the small little pleasures that the DTC would offer...

From the BC... to the Bimmer... and 18 blissful years later... Smee and I look forward to renew our vows for the next 18...

18 till we die...

2

Pig Tail... and the Blue Rubber Band

It's good to be writing all the time... despite the vanishing act that I keep putting in on my blog space (www.fursatfriday.com) every now and then...

Well – some of my true friends always seem to care well to see me back in the my blog world... but for many others that see me randomly through my blog identity... what I write – **Cold... Rolled... Annealed... and Pickled...** is always what gives me utmost pleasure and proves to be my raison d'etre for the last many years... when I was dumped by bosses, brands and banter alike...

And then there is a lot that happens when I am not writing...

For example... the 3 times that I got sacked from my various jobs and companies in the last many years while the companies themselves were figuring how to sack themselves out...

I was sacked out of this Insurance company the first – in 2007... they were closing down their operations in India... so they found it important to shed some flab... not that I was peculiarly podgy or plump... but my exit looked good on their balance sheet... the accounts books turned crimson from red...

And my boss was next... so their books were back in black...

I was sacked out of this Communications Software Technology company – in 2009, exactly 2 years later... this time because I had sported a pig tail... my boss had asked me about this sleek little white haired appendix conspicously jutting out at the nape of my neck... tied down in a small blue rubber band...

I had said – this is the latest passing fancy of the bright eyed and bushy tailed metrosexuals like me... and the best thing to have happened to the rubber band industry in ages...

My boss had promptly ordered my exit... what with no explanation or advice that she gave me about how I would sport the rubber band, leave alone the pig tail... in all those job interviews that I would need to go to in search of my next life...

I was sacked a third time in 2011... this time because my big Computer Company got bought out by another small Computer Company half the size of the big one... but this time, it wasn't my pig tail and the rubber band... both of which I sported with aplomb...

And this time too, my boss had asked me... and this time, I was smarter... I had said – my pig tail is my religion... and my boss had left the topic untouched and unfinished all through the buy out and transition phase of my big Computer Company...

But I wasn't the only guy who got fired this time around... the CEO of the small Computer Company also got fired... not for a pig tail and a blue rubber band... but for his own brazen voracity for sensual pleasures which took the carnal route... and the small Computer Company had no way out, but to sack him... in English – we call this Sexual Harassment...

This small Computer Company has since been acquired by another French Computer Company of gallic (or is it garlic) proportions...

So, isn't this garlic... er... gallic company blessed... what with both the pig tail and the geeky casanova out of their balance sheets...

While getting sacked became a way of life in between putting this manuscript together... there was an unmistakable learning each time I was at the abattoir where the axe fell... the learning was to come back to what I enjoyed doing most... get back at the world with a vengeance... wiggle it away... laugh it off...

As Confucius say to the King of Lu in 500 BC... This Too Shall Pass!

Getting to buy the domain www.fursatfriday.com on Wordpress this time (earlier it was Blogger from Google) was surprisingly easy... for just 18 dollars annually...

I used to pay 10 dollars to Google for the same domain name but as fate would have it... I had failed to show up with my credit card in 2011... impoverished, as I was, with my frequent sackings and the curse of the pig tail... Google had confiscated my domain...

When I woke up and went to the domain... to my utter dismay I saw railway tickets... stainless steel cookware... aircraft engines and lingerie being sold... amongst other umpteen wares... I had thought my poor little electronic kingdom had been invaded and brought under the rule of some free-spirited Leftist dissident... only to discover that Google uses the same exact home page for all confiscated domains...

So much for austerity and aesthetics...

My newfound fascination to keep coming back to writing and retain the domain name has a lot to do with my pig tail and the blue rubber band... because each time I wore this fancy little fad at the back of my neck, I did something new and different...

Or at least I would like to believe, I did...

Like publishing C.R.A.P ...

800 000

3

Wrong Number

"Oh. I am sorry. I got the wrong number" said Manju...

B was unfazed... I am sure he would have heard this many times when Manju called him in the past... after all... who would know Manju after many years of togetherness as partners in life and crime called... matrimony...

Mohan (B), my friend and I were at our dinner last evening in our hotel in Chennai... In ordinary circumstances, I would not have given it another thought...

When you are 10 years and over in a loyal marriage to your wife... you do look forward to certain unexpected thrills in life – like a pleasant voice that you do not recognize over the phone... a voice that you would love to carry on a conversation with... meaningless or otherwise... it is also quite understandable that when you near or are at your mid life... like me... the disappointment is far heightened to hear and bear a woman on the other end of the line say what Manju just said...

It triggered all kinds of elliptical thoughts in me... what if Smee, my wife, were to call me all of a sudden on my phone at 8pm in the evening... especially when I am travelling... and say – *"Oh... I dialled a wrong number..."*

How would I bear the colossal burden of a realization of being a wrong number in my wife's life... have I always been a wrong number or is it only of late... worse still... am I only a number digitally documented in her mobile phone contact list... and what kind of a number am I... a whole number, an integer, a fraction or a figment of my wife's fancies...

I thought of my two young children and wondered what would they say when they came to know of this... they are at a stage where they are still grappling with the first 100 number count in the numeric table... they only know all the right numbers in life...

Their father being a wrong number... oh my goodness... I don't know how I will be able to handle that...

My thoughts went to all my friends whom I had 'informed' about my wedding in November 1997... many of them faithful ones, who had still, without an 'invitation'... travelled all the way from Delhi to Hyderabad... to witness the love and the vows that my wife and I exchanged on that fateful day that was to bind us in a commune... a bond that was deemed to be our destiny for togetherness till time without an end...

Or at least till a number – right or wrong - did us part...

At this twilight hour of my life, my thoughts toyed with certain uncertain alternatives... chances of another possible association, alliance or a second matrimony... dreadful all, particularly when I thought of having lived through the trials and turbulations of my first and the current one... which I thought, until the call came and went... was perched firmly on a blemish-less branch of my heart, mind and soul tree...

My thoughts went to the time when I had first failed keeping our dressing table in the most appropriate form that my wife's eye would approve... my aftershave, my hairbrush and my deodorant – my three worldly possessions to look and smell good in life... to keep my bearings and self-confidence in check so that I never ended up being a wrong number in anybody's life, leave alone my wife's... and the way all three of them used to lay scattered at the far reaching corners of the territories of the dressing table... till my wife taught me how to manage a dressing table more than ever... now that we were married and share the dressing table...

I thought I had changed... at least for the ever overcrowding dressing table's sake... that can't sure be the cause for me turning a wrong number...

I thought of all those good holidays that we took together... she with an over-arching disregard for time – particularly when you are on a holiday – when she and I wanted to have breakfast, call the cab or reach a spot of tourist attraction... and I being fully finicky about breakfast at 0744, cab at 0827 and reaching a spot of tourist attraction at 0933...

Well, could that have caused the wrong number...

Well this one definitely could not have contributed... we had signed a legal affidavit on a 100 rupee stamp paper very early in our marriage... we had had made this information informally public when we advertised in six mainstream dailies and other tabloids in the vernacular press... that come tsunamis, thunder, hailstorm or the scores of relatives that descend on us every now and then... I shall get to sleep on the right side of the bed... my bed... sorry our bed...

And umpteen other events, mannerisms or high jinks that could be possible conspirators for me suddenly turning a wrong number on my wife's call...

I recounted all my responsibilities that I live up to as a good husband... I summed up I do a decent job of the dressing table, the holidays, our bed or our children and all other things of prime importance in our collective lives...

I mustered enough courage to conclude... I can't be a wrong nu...

"Hello Smee"...

That was my wife calling... it's almost 7 this morning... I am in Chennai... she is getting ready to go to school... in Gurgaon... of course, she teaches there... she has been teaching me to change for the last few years...

After all I am not a wrong number... hope so...

"Ravi... how many times should I tell you to keep the dressing table clean... I can't seem to find my hairclip"...

I know where the hairclip is... my dear wife normally finds it where it normally should be... perilously hanging from her hair...

Smee... I love you... and you are my right number...

⸻ ⚬⚬⚬⚬⚬⚬ ⸻

4

The Kheer Theory...

The Child is the Father of man...

The child is 14... not a child any more... not a man still... hasn't definitely fathered anything yet...

But when he shared the **"Kheer Theory"** with me when he was half his age... 7 years ago... Krtin, my son, never thought he was sowing the seeds that would... one day not so far away... help him cherish the fruit...

As the family prepares for him to fly away from the nest... into a residential school for the next 4 years of his formative schooling... where his colleagues will be brown, black, white, yellow and from many different hues and shades... from more than 10 countries in the world...

I am reminded of the **Kheer Theory**... an unformatted understanding of worldly wisdom... of a 7 year old...

A blast from the past...

-----

*"So, did Mummy have **kheer*** before I was born?"*

*Kheer (n) – An Indian sweet delicacy that is cooked with rice in milk and garnished with spices and nuts and served as a dessert.

A question that all Indian parents dread to answer... especially if you have lived and grown up on an overdose of **Ramayana – one of the greatest epics in Indian mythology...**

While Kavya, my 5-year-old daughter asked this in all her innocence... I thought I could still goof my way through... or give her the usual story that parents of my stage of life gave their children when confronted with **"Papa, tell me how I was born..."**

As a bedtime read, I have always cherished this habit of putting my two children to sleep with stories from all over the place... including the fairy tales (of their mother and I... before we got married)... and the ghost stories (of their mother and I... after we got married)...

And of specific interest to them was Indian mythology... and Ramayana in particular... for it has many answers... to questions that have been asked... and to those that may never be asked...

Ages ago... **Rama** – the hero of Ramayana... was born, along with his 3 brothers, to the three queens of **Dasaratha**, the king of Ayodhya, in northern India... **Rama**, the eldest, was born to **Kausalyaa** – Dasaratha's first wife... **Bharata** was born to his second wife **Kaikeyi** and the twins **Lakshmana** and **Shatrughna** were born to **Sumitraa,** his third wife...

So Far... So Good...

What caught my daughter's intrigue was what the mothers had before the brothers were born...

Kheer...

Now... the legend has it that the king performed a ritual where he lit a sacrificial fire... towards the end of the penance, out sprang the fire god with a pot of ***kheer***... which was consumed by his three queens... albeit not in the same proportions... Kausalyaa had half the *kheer* and Sumitraa a half of the rest... Kaikeyi had a half of what was left... and perhaps did not like it much and passed it back to Sumitraa, who again had the rest...

And lo and behold... the princes were conceived...

And the most convenient answer to keep my daughter's interest alive in all things that are god-like and other humanly impossible enterprises like procreation, was to say... "Yes my dear... your mother had *kheer* before you were born"... I said in all earnestness...

If our mythological heroes were conceived after a commodious consumption of *kheer*, the answer is conclusive... and I could not be lying...

"But what do they eat in America? They don't have kheer there – right?"

Well – this answer was not to be found in Ramayana...

Nevertheless, for everything that is earthy or ethereal, Kavya's 7-year-old brother has the usual answers... especially if it is America... or China... or the land of Kangaroos and Kiwi birds...

"Of course, McDonalds, silly!"...

For my son, anything American was either Mickey Mouse or the Big Mac...

I would have thought with that one sweep of a masterstroke... my son had silenced all critics who ever questioned what mothers normally had in other parts of the world too... "Of course, McDonalds, silly!"...

The ubiquitous 'M'... for all Motherhood worldly...

But once India and America were comfortably dealt with... and culinary linkages firmly established with progeny... the attention shifted to other parts of the world...

Invariably... a 7-year-old is satiated only when the world took one complete spin on its axis...

"And in China?"... was the obvious next...

For the Instant Noodles generation that she belonged to, this wasn't difficult for my daughter to figure out...

That night... we tired ourselves out to sleep but not before clearly connecting all the cuisines of the world to the respective mothers in those geographies...

The next day I had walked them to the school bus stop... I thought the **kheer** had gone well through the active metabolism of two hyperactive children... and has been comfortably digested out...

"So, is that why children in different worlds are different? I am brown, there are white children,

and black, and fat and thin, and there are children
with red hair, and tall and short?"

My son announced to me... in one of the most
beautiful realities of life as seen by a 7 year old... a
world meaningfully diverse for a young child... which,
many of us, as adults, often tend to shun or shy
away... when we bring our prejudices to life and play...
when our tapes run when we see people different
than us... simply close doors to opportunities to make
this world a better place...

"Yes... silly... because their mothers had different
foods before they were born..."!

Krtin goes off early next month... takes new wings
to soar into newer skies... along with children (not so
children any more)... and with men (not so men yet)...

While he prepares to father bits and bobs...

5

Munna

Munna... my Man Friday for the last 10 days since I landed up in the land of promise and opportunity, MUMBAI... is a man of many episodes, takes and shots...

His life is an endless rhetoric of what Mumbai is... has been... and will ever be... for the countless teeming denizens like me who flock the city day in and out in search of life and its meaning...

"Apun idharich paaida hua" (I was born here) said Munna... the pride in his voice conveyed to me a bare simple fact... he made it clear that he is not an immigrant from up north in the country, like many

who have migrated and have literally seized the profession of driving people around (read - cabbies)...

Munna has been my chauffeur, city guide and mentor for on-boarding into Mumbai – with all its glory and glut... showing me around the places of interest for an immigrant... a house to live in... a school for my kids when they move in in about a month... lifespots in the 'Maximum City'... like the dance bars... the glitz and the glamour points... the theatre action... and more importantly the malls and the multiplexes for the urban rat in me...

MUMBAAAAAaaai...

For someone from Delhi who has lived all his life amongst spaces... Mumbai comes as a surreal shock, bordering on terror... A 10' by 10' bedroom is just enough for you to spread your feet so that your toes end up touching the wall in the front... not that I have grown longitudinally since I have come here... but someone who twists, curls, turns, somersaults through the night and ends up on the window ledge in the morning... bedroom space is of prime consequence...

That is... if you are fortunate and have a window in front of your bed... if you do, you could hang your feet out on the ledge... and if you happen to be on the 10th floor of a high rise like I have contracted to be... you could hang your feet down the window and hope a crow that you have wronged in its past life... doesn't drag you down...

Munna is nonchalant when he hears this... not that you did not have the intelligence to figure things out yourself... but with a little more time and familiarity I am sure I would hear Munna's words in my head – loud and clear...

"Saab, kya Taj Mahal mein rehne ko aaya kya? Mumbai mein to aisa ich makaan milta hai"... (Have you come to live in a palace? In Mumbai you only get houses of this order).

Got it Munna...

"Where do you live?" I ask him...

"Apun ka ek bahut bada building hai. Apun 3rd floor pe rehta hai"... (I live on the 3rd floor of a big building)...

Munna bought this place for his wife and two small little kids Saba and Ayaan a few years ago... in Thane... you see, he was a property broker in his past life... and before that, he was in the Oil Fields in Riyadh... then he was a gardener... and then he was the Personal Assistant for a Doctor – a heart specialist – at the Leelavati Hospital...

"Woh doctor na, bada accha doctor tha... dil ka doctor... bahut naamdaar... north ka tha... UP ka... vegetarian... kabhi kabhi apun ko bolta tha... Munna, yeh do Beer Baatli car mein chhupa ke rakhne ka... lekin bahut Gentleman tha"... (the doctor was a good man, he was from up north in UP... at times, he would

ask me to hide a couple of beer bottles in the car)...
Munna would describe the doctor...

Munna told me about the way the doctor invited to show him a bypass surgery on a big screen while he was performing one... *"Kya jaadu rehta in doctor logon ke haath mein Saab... Idhar se wire ghusaaya, udhar se nikaala... Aadhe ghante mein sab kuch khatam... Bole toh patient nai..."* (the doctor had magic in him... he would very effortlessly perform the surgery) said Munna...

Munna got philosophical yesterday... he started talking about his previous employer again... *"Apun ek din doctor se poocha... kya doctor saab, gareeb logon ko Heart Attack nahin hota kya?..."* (I asked the doctor once... don't the poor suffer a Heart Attack?)...

Munna described to me the doctor's reply... unadulterated, pure and the stark truth...

"Munna tera case dekh. Tereko dil mein dard hoyega na, tu kya karega? Aamrutaanjan lagayega aur lagaake so jaayega. Tu lucky hai to subah mein uthega. Aur bahut jyaada lucky hai to nai uthega. Tereko to pata bhi nahin lagega ki tu mara to Heart Attack se. Yeh jo paisawale hain na, inke paas paisa hota hai, dard hoyega to doctor ke paas jaayega. Tere paas kya hai. Tereko Heart Attack hoyega to seedhe Bhagwan ke paas jayega"... (The rich go to the doctors because they have money, but the poor go straight to God).

Conversations with Munna bring out not only the 'man in the mirror' for you... but Munna acts as the prism which filters the rut and rot... and projects the right hues for you to see... the choice is of course yours... as always...

Munna asked me one day... *"To Saab, tum idhar kya dhoondne aayele ho? Aamitabh Bacchan kadka aaya tha. Actor ban gayela hai. North se bhaiya log taxi driver ban ne ko aata hai. Tum kya karne ko aaye?"* (What have you come to Mumbai for)?

I thought for a while... They say, in Mumbai, you must talk like Mumbaikars... I said – *"Apun bhi kadka aayela hai. Apun ke wallet mein just 3 ATM cards, kuch Credit cards aur ek Naukri hai. Apun bhi idhar kuch banke dikhayega"*... (I will sure prove my worth in Mumbai)...

While I do that...

———～ⵓ◦ᴄᴇ⊶ᴏⵦᴇᴏ⊶ⵓ～———

6

What Language Do You Think In...?

"What language do you think in?"

The question rang out loud in my ears... a harmless question that I remember Aaveg, my dear friend from my days with my first employer a few moons ago... had asked the participants in a Team Building workshop that both of us were facilitating at the silver sands of the Ganga at Rishikesh... way back when we were younger...

The weeds in the wilderness may have got to him – I had thought at that time...

While Aaveg continues to be young... what with his 5 ft frame not relenting to any kind of linear growth... I have added many wrinkles since the question... add to his 'Forever Young' frame, his baritone... which always mesmerised the maidens... and prompted command and respect on most mortals... and showered fear on some occasions for those he chased on phone to return the Company money...

You see... Aaveg was a Credit Card Collector... well, not someone who collects credit cards... but Aaveg was a part of the most hated community of worms that does little to help the cause to create customer confidence and loyalty... he chased customers who did not pay their bills on their credit cards...

Aaveg was, of course... different... despite the demographic that he was invisible over the phone... and even otherwise because his work table measured 2.5 ft in height... the charm and spell that Aaveg's baritone cast on all the female customers is a legend in the chronicles of this employer of mine... and Aaveg would often tell many of those damsels – *"Sweety. I am glad you love my voice. But I love my money. When do I get it back?"*

Aaveg's baritone accompanied the question in my ears... I was driving in the pesky peak-hour Mumbai traffic earlier this week... I recalled the last time when the question haunted me... actually – each time I drove in the Delhi traffic...

In all these years that I have breathed the fumes while in the thick of the Delhi blow-horns... I always fretted and fumed in Punjabi... that has been my language for thinking and behaving...

A language particularly flowery, fit and flaunted in getting back at the world... Punjabi is the only language where the non-verbals are more accentuated than the words you use... a lack of vocabulary is often compensated by the reverence and respect for female relatives in the family – your family... my family... the neighbour's family... it doesn't actually matter as long as an explicit set of greetings to the mothers and sisters of the world are mouthed abundantly at the start... the middle... and the end of every sentence and wherever else appropriate...

Propriety of this linguistic armoury is at times amply moderated with real time weaponry including automatic guns... especially on occasions when the road actually belonged to you and someone else overtook your car by felony or faux pas...

The Mumbai traffic, on the contrary... I discovered early on in my life in this city... neither poses a threat to my thinking capability nor does it challenge my linguistic aptitude... in fact, you just sit at the wheel and hope that the big bang will happen soon and it will result in your car moving the next 4 and a half feet of the cemented concrete below the rubber...

They say driving in Mumbai is a very stoic faced... yet an engaging act... in the most emotive action of engaging your transmission between the first gear and the neutral... your face glows with glee when on that rare occasion your car manages an advance of 6 and a half feet in one go... you are elated – like when you soar high in a hot air balloon - when you are... in that brief moment when reason lapses, able to spring forward in the second gear...

Linguistic thinking or no thinking... driving in Mumbai is a silently endured ritual... you are resigned to a lane, a straight, curved, crooked or an arched lane, doesn't matter... with no challenge whatsoever... no pedestrian or a cyclist jumps in front of your car... not because there are no pedestrians or cyclists... but because there is no space between your bumper and the fender of the car in front... you can't switch lanes because there are cars in the other lanes which are also equally resigned to their own lanes... you can't take the arteries for shortcuts as there are literally no arteries for you to take... as all arteries are choked leading up to blue tarpaulined multi-level shanties... you can't race ahead of any other car because all other cars are invariably going to your destination... and you don't pull out guns if the lane on the right moves faster...

Sunil, my friend of many years ago... was amazed at the discipline that I was demonstrating while driving together to work that morning... he had seen a different 'me' in Delhi...

They say, if you own a Delhi Registration number on your car as I do... your infamy precedes you here in Mumbai...

I told Sunil – as matter-of-factedly as I could... that one should stick to one's lane.

And as if it was a tailor-made repartee... Sunil was ready – *"Toh mere bhai. Ab hame dilli waale sikhayenge ki Driving kya hoti hai!"* (so, we are now going to learn how to drive from the Delhiites?!)

Fame or infamy... Aaveg's question was very apt that morning... What would it be like thinking and behaving in Marathi while driving on the Mumbai roads...? or my mother tongue, Telugu...? or English... the Lingua Franca...? how would my behavior be different than when I think in Punjabi...? is it the tolerant Mumbaikar that is driving the Mumbai traffic or is it the traffic that drives the Mumbaikar to be tolerant and patient and observe fundamental rules of humanity in life...?

While you think about it in any language that you are fine with...

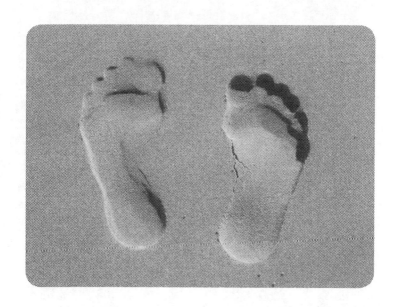

7

Pairi Pauna Paaji...

"Papa, why do we bend and touch the feet of our elders?"... asked Krtin, my 14 year old son...

We were returning from Surat... a 5 hour drive from Mumbai, where my parents live... and as has been customary all these years since my parents have had their grandchildren stepping into this world... this last Tuesday too, my children, my wife and I bent fairly forward, with all the spine that we could muster... while bidding them goodbye with a revered touch of feet...

Growing up in Delhi all my life... and in a multilingual culture called Punjabi... my adaptive intuition in all those years of my becoming... taught me to experience the art and science of 'touch-the-feet-of-the-elders' play out in myriad ways...

From the prostrate **'Saashtaanga Pranama'**, that Subbu – my Tamil friend and next door neighbour and his sister Gayathri used to strike... to Debabrata (Debu) my Bengali friend, getting down to his haunches and touching the right foot of his parents and elders... to some of my Marathi and Gujarati friends from the west of the country, faithfully resting on their knees and shower their reverence...

And my friend Balvinder (Happy)... who did his **'Pairi Pauna'** (touch your feet) with supreme devoutness and with least of bodily inconvenience to self and others... you see... touching feet in Punjabi is actually touching you somewhere slightly below your belt and a lot slightly above your knees...

Call that feet... it is convenient... bodily...

It took me nano-eras of growing up to get to the bottom of it all... well literally... as the bottom of the subject being the feet... but quite imprecisely a lot below the precise bottom the way we know in an anthropologically evolved human anatomy...

Well if that is about the bottom of beyond... or behind... the front is what is the essence of it all... the **'Sa-Ashta-Anga Pra-Nama'** that my friend Subbu used to deal... has a very scientific supposition behind it... not the same behind as the earlier behind... but a behind nonetheless...

Sa – along with and in a coordinated way...

Ashta Anga – with 8 parts of my body – my toes, my knees, my palms, my chest and my head touching the ground and thus when I am one with the elements...

Pra-Nama – I bow to you...

And, of course... I seek your blessings as I touch your feet... that's my purpose... and when I touch your feet, I bend low... low enough to make myself insignificant and make you the supreme giver...

Equipped with this *'Brahma Vigyaan'* (the supreme scientific knowledge)... I set out to dissect one of the most commonplace customs... the art of touching feet in conventional India and its own share of untold and must-not-be-told interpretations and implementations...

Particularly the consequences of the art of bending... as one must always bear the end of the bend in mind...

The young bend themselves forward most normally without bending their knees and facing the elder in front... and touch their feet... the right foot in many parts of the country, as that's the (right) side of the body which presumably has zillions of fast paced protons, electrons and neutrons carrying oodles of positive energy...

And the elder provisioned with this positive energy touches the head of the person in front... and makes that cosmic connect to transfer the protons, electrons and neutrons... to the person in front...

And this, accompanied by a plethora of implausible future postulations...

Sample this...

'Ayushmaan Bhava' (may you live long and defy life expectancy despite all your vices)...

And a step further – *'Chiranjeevi Bhava'* (may you be the immortal custodian of all that is happening today – and safely hand over the next few millennia to the next set of evolving generations of our race)...

May you grow rich (despite all the economic catastrophes that the world will see in the future)...

May you grow wise (than what is cosmo-genetically possible)...

And the best of it all if you are a married woman...

'Deergha Sumangali Bhava' (till death or alimony does you and your husband part... actually come to think of it... may you kick the bucket before your husband does (sic)... let the bugger endure your absence... as he had - your presence... life, and death, must be a continuum)...

'Putra Poutra Prapti Rastu' (may you bear children – preferably male... and predictably transfer your virility to them so that they have the right sexual orientation when they grow up and help further the clan)...

As a child, I had bent my back shedload of times to touch the feet of my uncles, aunts, their uncles and aunts, and all uncles and aunts that remotely had any mortal or combatal connect with me...

And the feat of touching feet was much amplified during wedding ceremonies in the family... particularly when all the uncles and aunts and everybody else even a day older to me... used to geopolitically flock together at the venue of the wedding... with a sole circumstantial vengeance to bless me... and anybody and everybody a day younger than them...

This... after the most engaging debate that preceded the green signal... if and whether they can rightfully bless me... after pulling out in thin air, the cosmo-spatial coordinates of the most unambiguous moment when I was born... the dissertation around meteors, stars, planets and their satellites that colluded and collided to ensure that... I was indeed younger than the ones that were blessing me...

Happy (Balvinder) and I have since seen many feet in many a soil... what with Happy now happily and conveniently (both bodily and soul-ly) making **Traunto in Canedda**, further up in the northern hemisphere – his more permanent home...

While Krtin will deal with his own interpretation... and implementation of 'touching-the-feet-of-the-elders' as his own growing up with adaptive intuition... my reverence to Happy will always be in my heart... and in his feet.. where his feet are... in Punjabi...

You see... **Happy is 47 days elder** to me...

Pairi Pauna... Happy Paaji...

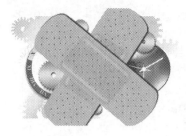

8

Humour, Pain and Sex... Vol 1

Humour, Pain and Sex... the 3 top grossers to hook your fish... Trust Me...

Not strictly in any order, the above... God comes a close fourth...

Now that you are hooked, let me drop the line...

In a 3 episode interlude... today, I shall talk about Pain...

As a twitterpated watchdog in the *Sixth Estate* (Social Media), my eyes water very often these days...

... Not because of the excessive staring into screens of all kinds and spending countless nano-hours when on WhatsApp, Facebook and my work email (strictly in that order)...

... Not because my Apple gadgets are neither 'Retina 4k Display' nor are ginormous...

... Not definitely because of an overdose in my body, of *'adrenocorticotropic'* hormone... okay – the hormone that helps run those tears down your mascaraed face, when you defend your hearth, your husband or humanity at large... particularly when attacked by your boss, your mother-in-law or your neighbour's spouse...

My eyes water heavy... and here's the reason why...

Out of my 1,600 Facebook friends... whose posts religiously appear in my scroll everyday... a 400 are perpetually *pained* by what they see of themselves in their profile picture and another 500, by their cover picture... and about half these friends are *pained* by both...

So they have this eternal *'khujli'* (itch, a psychologically advanced and a 'must-do-something-about-it-now' state of pain) to keep changing their pictures every now and then... sometimes 3 or 4 times a day... just to keep themselves engaged... with themselves...

And then there is a good number of these narcissists who are *pained* if there aren't enough 'likes' registered on their posts... would call up their friends and plead with them to click 'like' on their posts... this click of a 'like' works more wonders than **'ITCHGUARD'**... which alleviates all kinds of itch, more so in those parts, that you cannot scratch in public...

Some others among these would love comments... which manifest these days in animated emoticons... called emojis... and if you wrote comments in plain English, like I do... my friends are not only offended... but their emotional suffering auto elevates to Saffron (the next in degree to Green, Amber, Red)... **RAGS** status, if you will...

Some of these emoticons without exception, emotionally push you to the wall... you spend the next precious life minutes figuring out what they are actually wanting to convey... for example, I got this emoticon of a dancing damsel as a comment to one of my posts... I kept interpreting for the next half hour whether the damsel was in distress, disdain or discomfort... the dance itself was cross cultural... cutting somewhere in between Bhangra, Salsa and Asiko, a dance by the people of Douala in sub-Saharan Africa...

A significant number of my friends have a malefic lot of friends... on Facebook, of course... and a lot of them are known to many of us... now, if that in itself is not complicated enough, the pain gets multiplied...

particularly when one of them bitches about the boss... his boss... her boss... who also happened to be my boss, sometime in another life...

While it is a universal phenomenon that we all love to hate our bosses, but bitching about any boss... on Facebook... causes me immense *pain*... I have an unplumbed regard for all bosses, this side of the galaxy... I am one myself... bosses are avant-garde and worldly-wise sods from the same galactic coordinates as us... they are there in their roles as our bosses, because they have committed some colossal boo-boos in their lives... otherwise, they would not deserve us, to manage...

A good number of my friends are soulful and solo-lived... *pained* by their solitude, they take solace in sharing images and quotes and quips which legitimise their lonesomeness... take refuge in 'Power of Positivity'... and 'Steven Aitchison', who takes the cake in furthering this legit... take a look at your first 20 posts on your scroll on Facebook Home... I am sure you would notice Aitchison squalling sadness into your eyes... and those unstoppable tears onto your mascara...

Some people are genuinely *pained* by all that is happening around them... Facebook, or otherwise... I am peculiarly *pained* by my neighbour's attitude towards her husband and I... well... your neighbour could be a woman as well, right?

This neighbour of mine has a challenge managing her husband each time he and I go out binging in a pub near where we live... come on... **a man deserves a man's life**... and it *pains* me when my wife and she collude to drive the living daylights off us... principally and principle-ly after we have had a few you know what...

Pain...

Each time I experience *pain*... my heart goes out in empathy to all those who have similar friends as I, on Facebook... similar neighbours as I... similar bosses as I... similar solo lives... as I ???

Hmmm...

"Har Taraf Har Jagah Beshumaar Aadmi... Phir Bhi Tanhaaiyon Ka Shikaar Aadmi..." - *Nida Fazli (Urdu Poet)*... **(People everywhere around me... and I find myself alone)...**

Pain... thanks for staying hooked...

9

Humour, Pain and Sex... Vol 2

When you have sex on your mind all the time,
you simply... Go, and Write about it...!

When I posted the last episode on Pain on my
blog last Friday... I won the adulation of the ten
and a half comments and 28 likes on Facebook...
and a similar number on WhatsApp... what with my
musings in equal measure around both absurdity and
solemnness around Pain...

In this one... I thought I would like to train my lens on
Humour...

Sorry to disappoint those, who always have sex on
their minds...

"She married me because she likes my sense of humour... and I married her so that I could make her laugh about all the jokes I told her"... my wife agreed... till we got married...

Over the years, this motive of mine has driven me... the consolably not-so-good-looking-me... to become and be an "Enter-Trainer"... but it's true that I am only second since human evolution... Socrates was before me...

While "Enter-Trainer" is not the solo label that I have lived with, in my chosen professional space of Training, Education, Development et al... it helps...

"Why are you so self deprecating in presenting yourself?"... I often get this question after I introduce myself in the first 5 minutes of any Training programme that I run...

Consider this...

"My name is Ravi Kodukula... pause... the name is not going to be easy or difficult for you to forget or remember... pause... and here's the reason why... my name rhymes with one of the best brands in the FMCG world... pause... and if Coke drops out of Fortune 100, I would change my last name too... pause..."

Pause for effect... usually a sneer, a jeer, a boo or a moo... **Deja Moo** to be precise (we have heard that bull-crap before)...

But yes, I have lived with Coke, Koke, Koka, Kodak and a few other phonetic palindromes... and once I have had that initial connect with my audience... around how easy I am to deal with... it peels that first skin for me... off me...

I would think... one who laughs at oneself... has this vitality to consume the contemptuous charades of human existence... and secures a moral, licensed, high-minded nobility to laugh at the rest of the world...

That's the first 'sense' of humour... **TASTE...**

How does Humour taste? We sense humour through various senses... how oxymoronic... but till we know we can laugh at our own travesties of life, we haven't 'tasted' humour... we need to feel it on our skin... deep within the skin, in fact... and be comfortable about it... because if we are not, we give away the mural right to paint humour on others' skin...

Not too far away from the skin is the heart... it needs a **TOUCH** of humour to get that tingle... and you don't need to be a stand up comedian to cause that... just hit upon humour around communities of people... and you got a social buy in... because we humanlings have this idiosyncratic greed for umbilical symbolism... connect me to my community... and I say – yeah – that's like me... that's like my brother...

my spouse... my neighbour's spouse... Yeah... you TOUCH me...

And just imagine... when you were in school or college... and at 7am, you were sitting in your bed staring slightly into space... with no particular thought in your mind... and your father passes you buy... and he shakes his head... **PSST...** and he walks by...

Or, when you got married... and on a Sunday afternoon you are in front of the TV and watching the India Pakistan game... with the remote tied safely to the *'naada of your pajamas'* (the string that holds your pajamas together)... your wife passes you by... shakes her head...**PSST...** and she walks away...

The **SOUND** of despair in their **PSST...** just roll it in your voice box... under your teeth... with a twitch of your lips... make that sound now... and the **SOUND** of humour that the **PSST** tingles in your heart...

Trust me... it's decibelically better than a 'Ha-Ha'... 'Hee-Hee' or... 'Ho-Ho'... or all those emoticons on Social Media put together...

You don't have to flare your nostrils up every time somebody walks in and when you know the atmosphere is going to liven up... when you see laughter in a public place... when you hear a bunch of girls grinning... when you witness a man going down on his knees in a restaurant to propose to his date...

You **SMELL** humour... because you can well imagine what this guy on his knees is getting into... and knowingly... and you pardon him for his follies... for that instant... and for the rest of his life...

Because you have been there before... Déjà Vu...

Or is it **Deja Chu**********... the feeling of having met yourself before... the **SIGHT** of Humour...?

 Be Like Bill

10

Humour, Pain and Sex... Vol 3

This is Bill...

Bill has sex with several partners... both men and women... every day... and every night... and every in between...

Bill does not tell his partners about one another...

Bill is Smart...

BE LIKE Bill !!

https://en.wikipedia.org/wiki/Be_like_Bill

Depression is fast becoming obscenely pandemic... and my psychiatrist friends are laughing all the way to the bank...

In the last two episodes... since my friends sniffed a possibility of Humour, Pain and Sex trilogy, 3 of them went into depression when I posted the second episode last Friday on my blog... the obvious reason, they confided in a psychiatrist friend of mine – I had parked Sex for the last of the trilogy...

Another 7 sent me anticipatory WhatsApp... that I should not fail them... how they were pinning all their hopes on the concluding piece so that they could revive romance in their relationships... reignite that flame in their dying sex lives... 3 of them ordered global condoms on www.alibaba.com ... one of them incidentally started e-dating **Morgiana** on the site in anticipation...

2 of them threatened me of unimaginable consequences if their worlds were to collapse if I did not conclude what I started... how there was no escape route...

Friends... believe me... I am not into **EROTICA**... that's a specialist genre reserved for social anthropologists starting with the critics of *Swami Vatsyayana*... and ending with *Clinton and Cosby*...

Bill...

When I was growing up as a father, a few years ago when my son was born... my good friend **Brijendra Kathuria** gave me a parting gift when I was leaving one of my umpteen employers of the past... with whom I spent just about seven months...

I was thrown out of the firm, as I was a cultural misfit...

Brij feared I might be an equal failure... socially, culturally, fatherly - a misfit... if he did not do something about it fast... he gave me Bill Cosby's parental musings all put into a book – ***FATHERHOOD...***

Bill impressed me to no end... at his wittiest, wisest and warmest, Bill Cosby came across much more waggish than a few of his TV Series that I had seen when I was just about growing up myself... ***A Different World... The Cosby Show...*** and I was particularly fascinated how he dealt with children in most of his shows...

The book did teach me a few things... and I started dreaming of how I would ever raise my own son... and later my daughter who was to follow him... my most dreaded fear was of how I would ever have my first conversation with them around sex... at what stage and age of their lives... what the physical setting would be... will that be a monologue... or would they respond... will I be the right one to talk to my daughter about sex... or will her mother do the talking...

More questions than answers... my readiness on this task, was far from **Green**... it was deep **Saffron**...

And when the day dawned, just over a year ago... we were on the road... I was driving and my son was up with his head out of the sunroof, beating the hell out of the wind on the Bandra-Worli Sealink... when he heard, in all the gusto of the wind... the RJ on Red FM 93.5 talking about *Vicky Donor and the Sperm*...

Krtin... my son, bobbed his head back in... and asked me the most stupefying question – *"Papa, what is a Sperm?"*

The boys must have been talking of all the jargon and the accompanying slanguage that one learns in early adolescence... I did when I was his age... at 13, most questions around sex are disruptively playful... yet, wilfully innocuous...

And yet, when I was 13, I never asked my questions of my father... nor did he willingly disrupt any natural convention of learning about sex... friends had fair means, not enough to cause any hulking illumination around the subject... my biology teacher was overtly starched when dealing with the chapter on **'Reproduction'**... what with all those salacious glances that we boys would throw at each other and the girls in the class... Doordarshan had its favourite taboos – and Sex topped the list... *Penthouse and Playboy were expensive...*

However, that first conversation with my son a year ago, was seamless... the most dreaded moment of my life was smoothly melted by the RJ, playing the catalyst... the wind played along... my offer to finally answer my son's first ever existential question of his life which he had been asking his mother and I for a long time – *Papa, how did I come into Mummy's Tummy*... was **NOW**...

And yet, when I explained the technical process in the most demystifying way... I was met with a raw smile – Papa I already know that...!

At least Krtin's response was less wounding than a video doing its rounds on the *Sixth Estate* these days... where the father clears his throat twice and says to his son, who is nonchalantly thumbing his smartphone... son – let's talk about Sex... and the son's instant response without looking up from his screen – so, what do you want to know about it, Papa...???

My father would have thought, I was on some wildering weed...

Not more gut-wrenching and mind-reading than **Google Baba** though...

Google Grass, the weed that they feed into Google Baba, threw up these two most popular, maybe most Googled, names when I did some G-surfing on Bill this morning... I found Clinton and Cosby in the Top

2... Gates was inconspicuously lost somewhere in the middle...

With all the legal battles Cosby fights around longstanding sexual harassment allegations... all of which he has vehemently denied with a 1 million dollar bail in July 2015... Clinton continues to give the other Clinton what he has given her in the last many years... **HEADACHE...**

In 2016, Hillary continues to be devastatingly plagued by Monica's pledge about her Presidential candidacy... Monica is pretty clear... she is not going to vote for Hillary... her reason – the last time, she stepped into anything to do with American Presidency... it left a pretty bad taste in her mouth...

Now, that might cause some geopolitical imbalance if Hillary were to lose by that just one vote... the Indian American bonds – promissory or otherwise – built so laboriously by Obama and his democrats... might just become fragile once more...

Time for some Indo-American intercourse... er... collective introspection...

In the meantime... YOU... Stay Smart...

BE LIKE Bill...

11

The Pajero Arrives

"You tell me this is a Real Estate investment and you want me to believe that crap...", roared Smee...

She looks amazing when she is angry... and sounds even better...!

It's good to be home! And no...I am not, an inch... hinting at how my wife occasionally treats me on my homecoming...

But today, my homecoming was indeed to do with a do or die of our relationship... i.e. - my wife's and mine... Of late, Smee has been amassing exquisite know-how on Real Estate and any hint at a possible discussion around matters of brick, mortar, Italian marble and Indian Hindware... meets with a heightened, insinuated, calculated and an informed outpour... with an 'I-know-more-than-thou-and-the-entire-cosmos' kind of a look, my wife brings her soul into Real Estate conversations...

Only that... this latest uproar was around my newest real estate acquisition...

"Are you serious? You are hardly going to be in that car for more than an hour every day and you drowned a fortune into this iron and plastic. And that doesn't look half as masculine and endearing as the Ford Endeavour?" stormed Smee, after a pause...

I tried explaining to her. "Mitsubishi Pajero" is named after Leopardus Pajeros, the Pampas Cat... which inhabits the Patagonia plateau region in southern Argentina... the first Pajero prototype was unveiled at the Tokyo Motor Show in November 1973... the Pajero II prototype followed in 1978, five years later... Mitsubishi's aim was to create more of a recreational vehicle, and not just an SUV... the locally-built Sports Utility Vehicle (SUV), by our own Hindustan Motors, which has successfully transported the likes of the Prime Ministers and the Presidents of our great nation... and how now that the Pajero is a perfect fit for uneven Indian roads as well as the slow-moving urban traffic... With a powerful engine, the diesel-driven vehicle offers good mileage and high top-speed... The off-roader is suitable for long journeys and can easily accommodate a family of seven people...

Though not in the least that my wife and I would have an interest in expanding the family from where we are, to a family of seven... just because the leopard is in...

My wife launched into a tirade of expletives... including how sad the Pajero looks... and how unexciting the roar of the engine is... compared to the other trucks like the Endeavour or the Tata Safari that she had sat in with me while we were test driving a host of the SUVs available in the Indian car market... half of which are epitomes of third world dumping... which come to you at double the price and half the features... than their cousins in Europe or North America...

The features of the Pajero did not seem to strike a chord with Smita... I tried the emotional angle... I talked to her about the first time when I, as a mere 17 year old, sat in the Pajero for the first time in my life... in Baghdad where my father was posted in 1985... and how I had always nourished this dream of owning the Leopard Pajero, the Pampas Cat... for the last many years... and how one lives only once... and how I have slogged all these years to redeem my dream...

The histrionics always worked... in the past... and now... Smee seemed to relent...

But she would not give up the last yard and a half...

"But tell me something – have you ever seen a Corporate Executive driving to work in a Pajero...?" she asked sheepishly...

I knew I was closing in on the kill... this was it... this was my chance...

"Wouldn't you want your dear husband to set a Corporate Example by being the first to drive to work in the Pajero...? a sporty white haired man stepping down the footboard from behind the majestic wheel of the big cat SUV... and admiration pouring in from all other cars parked around... a slight bow... a sleek applause... Just imagine".

I held her hand in mine and stretched our hands towards the horizon from our sea view balcony... the sun was just ducking down into the west... down 10 floors below in the parking lot, was the black and silver Pajero... standing proud amongst all other mortal cars...

Smee looked at the car... and into my eyes the next instant... her look reflected all the good and the hard times that we have lived through over the many years that we have been together... she touched my cheek... her soft touch always sends a lump down my throat... even after all these years of our togetherness... more than anything else, her look assured me of her approval of my latest real estate acquisition...

In that one instant she had approved of my righteousness to own the Pajero... she had confirmed all my hard work all these 20 years that I have been gainfully engaged with fooling a few business houses with what I can do in my various jobs that I held with them... and all these 25 years after Baghdad, that I have wishfully pledged to own the car... with that one look she had sanctioned my ownership of my latest "Real Estate"...

Yes... Pajero... here I come...

12

The Terminal

Viktor Navorski (Tom Hanks - The Terminal - Steven Spielberg - Dreamworks Pictures - 2004)... was dismayed at the Immigration Officials' decision to deny him entry into the United States of America... Viktor had a valid visa – which was duly invalidated because of a revolution – a coup followed by war in his home country Krakozhia... he had a purpose while in New York – of that of getting an autograph from a Jazz musician that his father adored... Viktor spends the next few months at the JFK.

That was in 2004... Fiction with added glamour (read Catherine Zeta Jones in the female lead) – in a Hollywood studio...

Ravi Kodukula (name unchanged)... was distraught at nature's wrath and fury... the Snopocalypse this weekend in North East America grounded him just about 50 miles away from JFK – at the Newark Liberty International Airport... Ravi had a valid visa into the US of A and had a valid citizenship of a country that exists in real time (at least until this went to press)... Ravi had a purpose to get back into India – just to be back home...!

Real Time... Fact Based, Experiential Exploit of having spent 28 hours stranded at Newark Terminal B and cozying himself in front of Restrooms at Level 2...

I thought the best way to spend my time is to perch myself directly in front of the loos... I had two objectives... I would like to be the first to use the loo once the Mexican woman cleaning the restrooms left the area and... two and more important... do some incisive observation of loo behaviours of my fellow humanlings across continents...

Needless to say, I was rewarded immediate opportunities of the wild kind as soon as I made myself comfortable... with a Jet Airways blanket that covered my prostrate self and with my 2 bags full of imported impediments... including my brother-in-law's new MacBook Pro... I settled my gaze on some of the first arrivals into what was to be my lair for the next few hours...

The first arrivals at the loo... who else – but all our Gujju-Bens?

With the US census last week throwing up half the New Jersey natives to be half Gujarati... well, the Gujjus have been here 3 generations and some of them would have done some Americans – most definitely... the Newark airport terminal full of stranded passengers so obviously comprised of Gujaratis – the Patels... the Shahs... and the Desais then...

They came in droves... the purpose – visit motherland... wedding season back in Ahmedabad, Valsad, Vapi, Surat and Baroda... we had Meenal and Rupal and Jigness in the flight – all of whom were reluctant party to this embattled antipathy in getting married in India... but... What to do? If you have to go, you have to go...!

So, they came... and when they come, they have all got to come together... all dressed in sarees worn the Gujarati way and with heavy waist length woollen jackets on top... and with no warmth and protection below the waist except the thin saree and whatever gets worn below the saree... they have to come again... and again... and keep coming all the while...

And when they come, Jigness (Patel) is always in tow... They say 'Bens' must never leave without their 'Bhais' in Gujju land... Jigness had to show them the way to the restrooms – written on overhead boards in Spanish and at places – wherever there were Gujaratis in the Terminal – in English too... not that it would make any discernable difference, but shocker of surprises, Jigness could read English... he had helped father Patel put up the boards last summer, in front of their motel on the New Jersey turnpike... one of the boards was 'Restrooms'...

And while the first gaggle of Gujjus were working out their Khakras, Theplas and Dhoklas inside... there was another set that was working the same stuff out – outside the restrooms... this set of 'Bens' was from the Air India flight which was also grounded at the same time... this kind of compounded the Air India problem as the already 'Thin Air' in the Terminal was suddenly upgraded to level 2 'Rare Air'...!

Then came the Nordics... an SAS flight to Stockholm was grounded too... they have to come together in families – I mean, whosoever has been lucky and have been able to make a family despite the cold i.e.... mama in the lead... papa right behind and 3 tall, blond, blue eyed kiddos with equitable body proportions... and longish faces – genetic, of course...

And nothing to do with their inability to hunt down a restroom the conventional way... the process which the Nordics adopt is a little different than the Gujjus – you see... they don't have a Jigness with them who could read English... and Spanish is too far down south and hot for them...

So, they come smelling the loo... wouldn't they want to put their long noses to use...? and come, they do, as a family because when they go to hotter climates than what they are used to... half of them suffer from running noses... so, somebody in the family must be able to nurture a normal nose and help them smell the restroom...

Then there was this French couple... *Ou, sont-ils Belges...?*! They were on the same flight as I - to Brussels... despite their latin orientation to languages, they continued to ignore the boards that indicated restrooms... somehow they figured out that both the Men's and the Women's must be somewhere together... lost in smooching away to gallic (or was it garlic) proportions... the couple stumbled upon the Gujjus and the Nordics all waiting outside the loos...

By now, the Mexican worker woman had decided to go about her job of cleaning the toilets irrespective of the presence of an international delegation... un-aesthetically holding parts of their anatomy so that they don't give way to nature's beckoning... and which was condemning her timing to clean the loos...

"If you have to go, you have to go"... she blew something hot in Spanish, which was slightly higher in decibels than a shrill of a hungry baby shaken up from deep sleep and a wee bit lower than a Zulu war cry...

At least the Nordics scampered off – more out of fear of their lives if this woman were to become any more aesthetically ballistic... the French couple continued to

be in an oblivious embrace and all other smells and
sounds around them seemed to be so distant...

By the time the cleaning reached its end, the Air India
status was already at a threat of being upgraded to
level 3 – 'Hollow Air'... and I needed to survive the
Terminal to fight my flight back into India... I found
myself cozy-ness around the only coffee smelling
Starbucks on the ground floor... Ground coffee
beans always are more refreshing than 'ready to
biodegrade' dhoklas...

After 28 hours at Newark and another 8 hours at
Brussels, I finally made it back home on Wednesday...

And Viktor Navorski – I heard – has since made it safe
to Krakozhia...

—꒰꒰ᘏ⑅ᘏ꒱꒱—

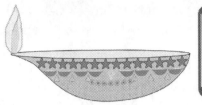

13

The FGMR Fatigue…

A smartphone… A decent network… WhatsApp… Facebook… Happy Diwali…!

Friend : Tried reaching you… met with an accident near the Hanuman Mandir… *Jaldi aaja* (come fast) please…

Reply : Thank you very much… Same to you and your family…

You suffer from an FGMR (Festive-Greeting-Message-Response) fatigue… when you are not sure who you last responded to... or which medium you used last to respond to greetings... when your thumb interminably toggles between 'WhatsApp'... EssMess (SMS - the regular text hub)... email... and the 'like' and 'comment' space on Facebook... Twitter... Hike Messenger... Hi5... Viber... Google+... phew... and you name it...

And then you decide to do poetic justice to the greetings... because your uniquely plagiarised message should be 'special and different' from the 'same exact' message that has been 'posted' by 543 people in a Fibonacci sequence just before you... and your dying need to add to your vainglorious vocabulary... that bizarre brew of your verbal expression that you have long saved for festive occasions... which you rightly think, is not... and should never have been... the prerogative of the lingua-purists... *like Ghalib, Momin, Meer or a Kodukula...*

Not so long ago... in my small little town called Chittaranjan in West Bengal... where I spent the first 7 years of my life... I recall my parents and their friends walking across to each other's homes to greet them on Diwali...

When I grew up a little more... I saw my father and his friends make firecrackers at home... not that the environmentalists or the fire department would approve of... but the home made firecrackers served as our staple for the festival... we never bought them from the cracker stores...

A little later in life... my friends and I made these firecrackers at home... our salvation into adolescence and a true belief that we stepped into bigger shoes...

In college... and away from home... queuing up at the omnipresent (yet, scarce) STD / ISD telephone booths and wait your turn to call home... particularly if you missed coming home for the festival...

In college and when you were in love... it was exchanging those Archies' Diwali Cards just so that you touch and feel the hand that gave you the paper cards, was a delight...

The first message that you got on that small little technological marvel called a 'pager' on Diwali was glory...

The first set of missed calls on your new mobile phone... and you hung up telling your friends that you will call them back from a landline and wish them on the festival, was prudence...

Landing your EssMess (SMS) 4 days before Diwali and with borrowed semantics that read... before the sun sets in the east... before the stars start falling into the sky... before the moon and mars collide... before the networks fall prey to congestion... 'I want to be the first with my Diwali wishes in your mobile'...

Seems so paleolithic today... but that wasn't a long time ago, all this...

Smartphones... qwerty keypads for mortal handiness... access to pre-fabricated 'messagery'... connect to the web...

And as my friend Onumita puts it... with the Social Media getting *'meherbaan'* (benevolent)... every *'gadha'* (ass – OK, donkey) is a *'pehelwaan'* (star)...

Sample this...

May your 'Festival of Lights' (noun... in short, Diwali or Deepawali), 'brighten up' (verb) your lives in as many ways possible (somewhere in between all parts of speech)...

Well – nothing wrong with that... except that my friend Navendu, grammatically challenged as he was in every language imaginable... for whom it was an effort putting together a straight sentence in the English language was nothing less than walking bare foot on a fire of burning coal... spun this one... bare footed... oops... bare minded...

That was, of course, when we were kids in school... Navendu has since been californicated into the cozy confines of San Jose in the Bay Area... and the dude is a motivational speaker...

For the more dramatically endowed, the festivals... particularly Diwali... bring in an opportunity to dust that old electronic dictionary on the web and pick out the choicest of adjectives and nouns... love, health, wealth, luck, good fortune, prosperity, peace, happiness, laughter, sparkling, blessed, blissful, tranquil, sweet memories, togetherness, fitness, abundance, satisfaction, **SAFE...**

SAFE ? the one thing that strikes me most about our festivals... about Diwali, Holi or the Elections in our electoral heartlands... is about this perennial concern with which my fellow human-lings wish for me to be SAFE... it's something like... I step out of home and I am going to be bombed... like it is festive terrorism... terrorism that borders on the benign... like - let me bomb you for the sheer love of you and humanity... and because you throw harmless water colours at people... and because you have decided to go to the polling booth and vote...

My personal safety status is consciously upgraded from Green to Amber... To Red... to Saffron... these days...

Now, weigh that up with the Brazilian Carnival... the Chinese New Year... the Thanksgiving in the US... or the traditional Ashes test at Lords... nobody warns you to be safe there... and not to fancy the Bull Fights in the latino world... you are always much safer than the bull's horns... unless, of course, you take the bull by its horns...

And then the mother of all appendices... Wish you and your Family... from the Khanna family... from the Kapoor family... from Chopra and family... or better still... from Aarghya, Aavani, Amruta and Ashwin Arora...

In all our festive greetings the family always browbeats itself into the equation... well, so much for a collectivist society that we are...

Now, Ashwin Arora... my bosom friend from my college days didn't show an iota of a promise that he was gifted to raise and rear his own self beyond the most obvious feat called existence... leave alone that of courting a woman and parenting children... and later skillfully master the most aesthetically alliterated family of four...

And don't miss the double Aa's in the kids' names... well that's exclusively to supply the kids with an added alphabetic cylinder to puff from... when they will always be called the first in their school ahead of the others with names starting with less earthly letters in the alphabet... like a Bb or a Cc... and give them the head start in life... whenever they engage in the 'potato in a spoon' race called life...

Well – if the words are upfront, the phrases are not far behind... loads of endless euphoria... sky fall of fireworks... mouth full of a confectionery store...

And no marks for guesses on the number of poets in the vernacular space... We are flowery in our mother tongue anyway and are universally flowery in Ghalib's Urduland...

Oh... Ok... I must respond to that Facebook post now...

"Thank you very much... Same to you and your family..."

14

Flat Pins in a Flat World...

This week, I broke all human barriers... and transgressed into a self-forbidden fortress called *'Nerd Castle'*... I got myself a *'Wireless Router'*...

For the uninitiated human mind... and mine, as such... the 'wireless router' would mean... when wired to a base personal computer or a telephone cable provided by my telephone or data network operator... and fixed at any forlorn location in my home... the router would allow me unlimited, uninterrupted and racy connect to the rest of the world on my laptop at any other non-fixed forlorn location within my home... and all other pitiful parts of my neighbourhood including Kookie's car on the right and Parvez's bar on the left of my home...

Unless, of course, I protected my 'wired' network with a security 'PassPhrase' that would protect me and all that I do in the virtual world... from Kookie's 16 year old son Bunty who nurtures his childhood dream to be the world's best 'hacker'... or from Johnnie Walker in Parvez's bar who keeps walking into every other network in the vicinity...

The 'wireless router' wouldn't start on Monday evening... predictably so... because of the 3 in-glorifying sins that 3 very intelligent people committed that evening... the guy in China who manufactured the cables and plugs for the wireless router... the sales person at Tata Croma at their newest outlet in my part of the world... and of course, me - the most supremely whip smart nerd, this side of the equator...

The first cardinal sin... the company that manufactured the AC cable that connects the router and the electric supply, attached a fancy plug at one end of it, that didn't resemble anything like the rest of the plugs in the household that would fit into the sockets on the walls... those that my wife and I laboriously built and installed brick by brick and socket by socket when we made our dream home a few years ago... when neither Thomas Friedman nor we, could imagine a flat world... with or without plugs with flat pins...

Guess what... the plug had flat pins...

For a Nerd, that would mean simply diving into a pile of plugs and sockets lying scattered (read stored) in all corners of all the 4 drawers of a chest of 24 drawers specially 'designed' to stack cables and wires (and all kinds of plugs and sockets) and everything else that even remotely resemble devices that help you connect to nerd-dom... the nerd would, with a whiff of white smoke and a hand gesture that would best resemble a Harry Potter Quiddich movement... pull out an adaptor / convertor that would transform flat pins into round pins... which then would eventually fit into the most normal human homes yet in India...

But, of course, for a mere human like me living in a yet modest human world... that meant waiting till the next morning when the shops reopened... or the evening when I could eventually make it to the shop... and hurl a few accusations at the guy who sold me the router with a flat pin plug... and didn't tell me about the flatness of it... which prevented me to get wired to the world through my wireless router the previous evening...

A loss of 24 precious hours of inactivity after shelling out a fortune... and the associated mental trauma, agony and a loss of self-esteem at the prospect of not even getting to the first step of a complicated 2 step DIY - Do It Yourself - process of setting up the router...

That was the second sin of the Monday evening on part of the sales guy... as a result of which, and for the nerdy partnership to continue and flourish between Croma and I... we together drafted and mapped an SOP - Standard Operating Process – as a part of the sales process at Croma... to ensure that the humans in a flat world are advised of the flatness of the pins on the plugs of electrical and electronic appliances that they buy to make their lives simple and convenient... and so that they do not have to bring their current home architecture down and choose to rebuild their homes to suit flat pin appliances...

And of course, the third foolish act was on my part... I should have anticipated... the possibility of a flat pinned plug in a flat world... especially since CIA, WTO, ISI and TLF (Thomas L. Friedman) have been conspiratorially warning me that everything manufactured in the rest of the world (read China), will be consumed in the more advanced world (read India)... including packaged breast milk...

The other part of the conspiracy theory was to make me buy accessories to the accessory that I bought... so, I bought the converter... that converts 230v of electric power into 9v... or is it the other way around... which was never a part of the original deal when I bought the router... a small price that I had to pay... as the global world continues to strip me down of the smells of the regular stuff from my backyard and gives me a taste of what I do not need... at uber-extra dollars...

Just imagine, I was happy with my round the corner coffee house, cinema, the modestly priced school and my round pin plugs and sockets... the global world gave me Starbucks, a Multiplex, a World School... and flat pinned plugs...

Well, at least the converter ensured that my wireless router is now wired... especially from the small personal park in front of my home, which is a pleasant place to be on Sunday evening... with a beer and a browser... and a laptop connected to the wireless router with a flat pinned plug...

It sure is flat... the world I mean... not the plug... or is it the beer?

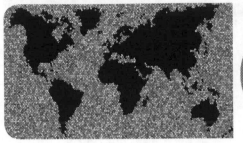 

15

The Earth Hour

My friend Hema is an environmental disaster... but since everything she says or does is bio-degradable, she is exempt from the wrath of the world...

This week we observe the 'Earth Hour'... and who do I hear it from the first? Hema, of course... Hema ensures everyone around her is kept informed and on more occasions than one in the recent past, she has been on a rampage... bullying people to do what is good for the environment... educating us on the consequences of not doing what she says... and most importantly, pricking me hard on my conscience... so that I write about her eco-insanity in public...

Because she says switching off all lights and electrical equipment – illuminating or otherwise – during the Earth Hour evening at 8.30pm… will reduce the warming of the globe considerably…

Can you imagine that… all lights… and Pinki's (Kookie's wife) prime-timed 16:9 plasma television… my friend Viv's all-weather ice-cube chiller which he needs to keep running and when Saturday nights are the special occasions for Scotch on the rocks… Pavan Chopra's 4 x 200 watt bulbs that he keeps burning in his lawn in the hope of a Guinness representative spotting him for the 'best-lawn-in-the-neighbourhood' award…

And most regrettably my 1024 x 768 pixeled laptop… connected to my 'now infamous' wireless router…

Because Hema tells me this is a global event… triggered by a set of 2 million loonies a few years ago in a despondent dwelling called Sydney in the most insignificant of geographies where every theme of life's existence is reversed or depleted… including the weather and the ozone layer…

Sydney… where they chose to experiment with what life would be without electric pumped lighting… maybe for an hour to start with… and try and empathise with the lesser mortals in most parts of the under-developed world like Gurgaon where I live… where life without electric pumped lighting is… a way of life anayway…

Because she tells me that 50 million more loonies joined the fad last year when it was unequivocally decided that March 28 should be the date when the changing seasons around the globe permit this to have the best visual impact... for the satellites, sent by the power-hungry nations into the upper space... to go clickety-click when in every town and city of the world, lights are switched off at this destined hour... and for them to beam back the images of how impactful this dark night 'show' has been...

Because she bullies me with a billion this year... in over 2,000 cities across 85 countries... and guess what... she tells me Delhi, Mumbai and Bengaluru have officially pledged to be a part of this fabulous light (or the lack of it) show... the power supply in these cities... and in many more that will join the pledge before this goes to press... will be 'officially' off...

So I ask Hema – what's new in my life? Little does Hema know that Gurgaon... has actually been a pioneer in a show like this... much before Sydney went gaga over this dark hour of humanity... Gurgaonites have long been bracing themselves against lightless lives... the lack of incandescent power – so to say...

We... the Gurgaonites... feel more powerful when the power is off... it's a true occasion to display to the rest of the world how sincerely we subscribe to the 'Me, Myself and My Mercedes' culture... the better illuminated the houses in the block are at the hour when there is a power failure... the bigger is our financial libido... because we are powered by a battery or a diesel-powered-electric-generator... which ironically pollute all the time... Earth Hour or not...

Pavan Chopra, my neighbour 7 houses down the row... has a power generator that powers all the 7 and a half Air-conditioners in his house... especially when DHBVNL– Dakshin Haryana Bijli Vitaran Nigam Limited (South Haryana Electricity Distribution Corporation – Limited)... the official electric power supply company that powers Chopra's house and all other houses in the neighbourhood, including mine... and one which is always Limited in its supply and distribution of electric power... decides to shed load (i.e. cut off the electric power)...

And as a symbol of solidarity with DHBVNL, Chopra has to shed load at the same time... *'toh main kiya Ravi ji... apne bathroom mein bhi AC, Shacey lagva lete hain... batti gayee to takleef nahin hogi'* (so, I thought Mr. Kodukula, I should install an AC in my bathroom too, so that when I am shedding my load, I will not be inconvenienced)...

So, what about the 'Earth Hour', Chopra?...

'Now, Ravi ji, when nature calls - you gotta answer... you gotta go, you gotta go'

And Pinki prides in her personal power generator to be able to power her 40 inch HD Ready Plasma

Television... and her 7.1 Home Theatre System... to watch the mono 'digital' TV channels that beam the umpteen Saas-Bahu serials... Pinki bought her HD ready TV because somebody told her the 'digital' transmission on all her Cable TV channels will soon be in the HD format... say in the next 17 years... and the 7.1 came free along with the TV...Big Picture – Big Sound... Prime Time Plasma...

'Earth Hour' - be damned...

But because Hema tells me... I have promised Hema... I will switch off the lights... and my modest inverter too... which can power a few lights and fans in the house... even if DHBVN Limited – with its Limited power supply – extends the 'Earth Hour' for more than an hour...

16

Kindly Adjust... Saar...

"The entry is from backside only... kindly adjust Saar..."

Girish Anna, the Security Chief at a premium Villa Complex in Bengaluru, ushered us in... from the **BACKSIDE...**

Not that he was physically endowed as was Adonis... as such, did not have too much to offer anyway, either from the frontside or the back... nor would Arun or I, have been sensually fascinated if an offer were to be made...

Enter we did, from the back of the complex... to get a glimpse of some spellbinding villas that Arun Menon, my friend, was planning to buy in the middle of the concrete paradise called Whitefield...

Siva, Girish Anna's 12 year old son also jumped on to the battery driven cart that took us to the back of the complex...

Arun had already been in the complex a few times earlier and he was taking me around on this occasion, to get my opinion on his decision... he had known Siva from his previous visits, and struck an easy conversation with him... in English... the only language that was the common connect between them both... Arun – because of his orientation to the language through his daily interactions with customers in his global role in his global firm... and Siva - as he himself proudly proclaimed, "I study in an English school..."

"Mummy ne bola hai ke mujhe Inglis seekhna hai" (Mummy said – I must learn English)...

Little Aarti's words still ring in my ears... years after I had taught her in 2008... at a school, which she may never have imagined that she would go to... learn with peers that she never thought that she would vie with... at an age when many kids, in more fortunate circumstances, would have already started scripting some early achievements in life...

But for Aarti, all of 9 years of age... my makeshift home school for the less privileged... in my lobby at my 'Kothi', in Palam Vihar, Gurgaon, was her first school in life... with her co-learners aged 6, 7, 11, 12 and 14... and with her biggest achievement in life to date... her ability to say an unblemished and right-accented 'Good Evening, Sir' to me in English, when she would come into my class at 6.30 in the evening... for many evenings in a row...

I recall I had started 'talking' in English when I was in my college... my schooling was in a 'Linguistic Minority' educational institution in Delhi... where the medium of education was definitely English... but where you had to take to the vernacular – in my case, Telugu, my mother tongue... as a third language to complete the scholastic curriculum...

My school, where I spent the next 10 years, gave my parents, my 2 sisters and I, just what we expected from it...

An infrastructure, decent enough to hold the roof when it rained (though on occasions we had to suspend classes because the classrooms got flooded... because of the leaks in the tin roof)...

Peers, who had similar means and resources to wade through life's waters... it was never enough... but of course, we had never known what was to have 'enough'...

Faculty which was learned enough to cause a difference in our lives... and importantly, with a defining urge to give more to their next generation, what they could themselves not get when they were growing up...

My school skilled me early in life in the English language... I had won essay writing competitions in the class... at times, at the school level... and on some occasions, at an inter-school level too... I was almost always on top... to the extent that I had topped in English and Telugu in my 10th grade (I was second in my class in Hindi)... and topped in English in the 12th grade...

But the one thing that I could never get myself to do was to stand up and talk in English... most of my communication was in Hindi... and English remained a language where I could prove my prowess only when I wrote...

Talking in English was a challenge in the college too... I just didn't have the confidence... and when I landed up in the Hotel Management School, I ended up faring worse... here, the 'gift of the gab'... and in English at that, was the clincher in most deals... including shaking hands with the most average looking girl in the class... left a streak or a smell of the English language...

I took the first steps towards the language in its most holistic form of both writing and talking... only in my work life, much later in life... a gradual happening and no miracle though... when I stood up and talked to thousands of my colleagues, my peers, my Trainees most often... over the years that I have been in the

Learning, Training, Development, Education space...
a language that I have, over the years, developed a
fondness for... which, today, in retrospect, seems like I
was never challenged with...

Aarti has since travelled through a journey in English
for the last several years... her parents are the
neighborhood local launderers... they press clothes...
earn 4 rupees for every piece of cloth that they
press...

Aarti's mother wanted her to adopt English as she
wanted her daughter to crack it big in life... *finitely
bigger than what she could...*

When I taught her for almost a year, 8 years ago,
Aarti was frail... under-nourished... she looked 5 while
she was 9 years of age...

But Aarti had dreams in her eyes... a steely resolve...
to turn her mother's dream true... learn English... do
something big... *definitely bigger than what her
mother could do...*

I was a part of her journey for a short while... till my
wife placed her in a more regular school in Gurgaon,
that she was working with, pro bono... I hear Aarti is
doing well...

Girish Anna never enrolled in a school... never spoke, read or wrote another language than Kannada all his life...

Siva, his 12 year old son, speaks English because his life depends on it...

And English – the lingua franca that cuts across the length and breadth of the country... the medium that opens up more opportunities for people to reach across and grab the globe... the only channel that propels better financial fortunes for a salaried existence in the country... and a path to a global citizenship...

Siva is the next generation start-up star in the making... in Koramangala... Bengaluru...

Until then... kindly adjust Saar... with Girish Anna's Backside entry...

17

Lucky… Just Got Unlucky…

My childhood friend and my ex near door neighbour from Delhi NCR… Lakhwinderjeet (**Lucky**)… gave me a frantic call this afternoon…

"Panga ho gaya, Kodu… Kejriwaal ne waat laga dee…" (Kejriwal has put me in some serious trouble… Kodu…)

Since the time Lucky and I were mere 9 year olds… we had this extreme fascination to call each other by a variety of names… we possessed a semitic and semantic prowess to invent and reinvent the way we called each other…

And then our other friends and adversaries would have a field day calling us by names... better and worse... till the time when we were 18 and we just got tired of coming up with new names...

That was when *Kodu, Kodak, Koke, Koka Kola*... and many other names that Lucky and I invented for me... came to be stuck with me a lot more permanently...

And then Kavya, my 12 year old daughter... who keeps coming back to me every now and asks me two of her favourite questions... how we came to be **Kodukula** and how desperately she wants to change her last name... for obvious reasons that she gets called Coca Cola...

The etymology of the Kodukula clan is easier for me to explain... primarily because of the certitude with which I can trace my family tree back to about 500 years...

You see, ***"KODUKU"*** in my native tongue Telugu, means 'son' in English... ***"KODUKULU"*** is plural... and ***"KODUKULA"*** is an adjective...

The origins of the clan must have been a perfunctory phenomenon in the making, some definitive period in the past... and owing to a time warped **'Yang'** flavour more than the **'Yin'** that some of my fore-parents had... with no forbearance around their virility, they had produced more sons than they could foresee...

And like the Indians that Columbus and Vespucci discovered a few hundred years ago, in the west of the pond called the Atlantic... and whose last names were etymologically assigned based on their visual aesthetics... like *'Anoki Bluefeather'* or *'Apisi Rednose'*... my family last name came to be **KODUKULA...** the family which has many sons...

My *'**Vamsa-vruksham**'* (family tree), in recent times though, never showed as many sons on its subsequent branches since that big-bang (sic)... but it's always more testing, explaining to Kavya – why she is in a unique disposition to be able to change her last name...

One – being a girl and when she grows to be a woman and gets married... she has an **OPTION** to change her last name or use a double-barrelled last name like a Kapoor-Khan... or she becomes a *'Phunsuk Wangdoo'* from a *'Ranchhordas Chhanchhad'*... https://en.wikipedia.org/wiki/3_Idiots and nobody would even question her decision...

But more than the fascination that Lucky, my childhood friend, had for names... his **magnetism for the number 9** kept Lucky and I more intrigued as we grew up...

"We became friends when we were 9"... Lucky would say with ample endearment... more so, when both of us are down on a few measures of **Old Monk** https://en.wikipedia.org/wiki/Old_Monk... somehow, we habitually found a spiritual connect between our hearts and our livers... Lucky would often say whenever we met... *"Chal... aaj phir apne Punjabi liver ko daav pe lagaate hain"* (let's put our Punjabi livers to test)...

Lucky could never embrace Telugu, my mother tongue... he would always make a hash of the few phrases that I had taught him fairly early on... I gave up one day when he used a Telugu phrase with a Punjabi accent in front of my parents... a phrase that was meant for boys... boys in their prime pubescence... and for unadulterated reasons, that adult phrase cannot be reproduced here... neither in Telugu... nor in Lucky's Telugu with a Punjabi accent...

Instead... I embraced Lucky's Punjabi liver... and his penchant for the number 9...

Lucky's roll number in the class was 9 ever since he went to school first... that remained so for quite a while... I joined him in Grade 4 when I moved to Delhi... my roll number was 21 for a long time...

Not that the roll numbers were anything to do with our eternal chuddy-buddy-ship... but both of us usually ended up sitting next to each other... in the 9th row... and as luck and Lucky would have it... the last row and leaning against the wall... entirely against my volition, but for my love for Lucky...

Lucky was born on 2-1-1968 (2nd January)... and if you added all these numbers together down to the last single digit, they added up to 9... Lucky would do anything new on a date that added up to a 9 – say the 27th, 18th or 9th... he even landed up in his first job on a Sunday... hoping at least that the Security Guard would be dozing inside the office and would open the doors... that was on 5th February a few moons ago... the 36th day of the year...

Lucky... like all Punjabis of his stage of life... what with one wife, two adolescent kids, and with **'Me, Myself and my Mruti (Maruti Suzuki) and my Mursary (Mercedes Benz)'** writ large on his patio of his 'kothi' in DLF Gurgaon... has very meticulously etched the numbers on his cars... DL 4C xx 4518 (the parrot green Maruti Gypsy) and HR 26 xx 3636 (the tomato red Mercedes ML250)... Lucky paid a pretty heavy sum to the Gurgaon RTO for the registration number of this tomato red Mercedes... **his car registration number is world famous in Gurgaon...**

...This afternoon... *"kee hoya Lucky?"*... (What happened, Lucky?)...

Lucky whimpered with panic in his tone... "Yaar... from 1st January 2016, you can only drive cars with odd and even number registration plates on alternate days in Delhi... *meri to lag gayee"*...

I took out my calculator and translated the import of his statement into numbers... the last 4 digits of both his cars add up to 9... down to the last single digit... that would mean Lucky can drive both his cars on the same day... and on alternate days, both his cars would adorn the patio of his 'kothi' in DLF Gurgaon...

"Sahi mein yaar... teri to lag gayee" (truly my friend... you are screwed mighty unlucky, Lucky)...

And knowing Lucky and the infamy of the world called Delhi NCR... Lucky would do some **'Jugaad'** at the Gurgaon RTO... trust me...

Because, when caught on the wrong side of the law, Lucky would always pose this existential question of anybody who will sit right up and take note... *"Tu nahin jaanta main koun hoon?"* (don't you know who I am?)...

You see, Lucky's uncle's maternal aunt's first cousin's son's sister is Kejriwal's adopted brother's aunt's grandmother's 3rd niece's 4th cousin...

While Lucky figures out his next steps...

—⁓⁓⌾⌾⁓⁓—

18

The New Year Card

"Ghar pahunchte hi chitthi likhna... aur Mamaji ko aur baaki padosiyon ko "Happy New Year" bol dena... is baar main Card nahin bhejoonga..." (write a letter when you reach home... and wish the entire neighbrhood on my behalf... this year, I won't be sending any greeting cards...)

My friend Lucky and I had just seen off Lucky's cousins at the Old Delhi Railway Station... the cousins had come in from Jalandhar for a family wedding in Delhi...

While Lucky and I customarily did most of the stuff together... this particular joint send off that day had a macho motive in it for me... a possible hope...

Simmy (Simran), one of the 3 cousins, and I had grown cozy close together over the last week or so during the wedding... and the scene at the station was sombre... bordering on... well – quite emotionally inexplicable - this soulful separation with Simran...

Simran was fortunately inside the train... it was December 1991... *Raj and Simran (Dilwale Dulhaniya Le Jayenge) happened later in life...* this was about my Simran... Simmy...

Simmy went off, and we never met again... we wrote a lot of letteres to each other... and sent each other a lot of greeting cards too... I had told Lucky of my crush for her after many years... after that fateful farewell at the Delhi station... a quarter of a century ago... almost...

A clichéd, mandatory rant, this – **write a letter when you reach home...** an inescapable sight at most windows of trains and buses before they left their stations... platforms teeming with more relatives to see passengers off than the actual passengers themselves... with a last piece of advice or a piece of mind from the elderly to the young... *acchi tarah padhaayi karna... mummy paapa ko tang mat karna...* (study well... don't trouble your parents)... the revered touch of feet... the last minute hug, with a laugh, weep or a cry... till the minute the train pulled off from the station...

Write a letter - I did many... one of my early recollections of writing letters was one that I wrote to my father... while he was the one who introduced me to letter writing, ironically, I wrote my first letter at the age of ten – to him... he was away doing his Bachelors in Arts in a different town for a couple of months... and our only medium of communication was through letters...

As I wrote more letters in my growing up years, I discovered that this was a class act... and had an unqualified hierarchy in my family... keeping the world informed of important events and worldly happenings was always the Head of the Family – my father... anything endearing, particularly asking relatives to come over and stay with us during holidays, or letting them know that we would be coming over, was unmistakably my mother... letting my friends and cousins know of the windward and wayward ways of life, was always I...

The choice of letters - what to write on - itself had a pecking order... a short 'informative' message would be on the *10 paisa Post Card*... a little longish emotional outpour – with a prologue, epilogue and everything in between was a *25 paisa Inland Letter* (a queer 1-page-and-a-half-when-folded-and-sealed kind)... if you had to write a story which ran into pages, you could use the *50 paisa stamp affixed*

Post Cover envelope, yellow in colour... or maybe an envelope of your choice...

A letter to an overseas friend needed a ***2 rupee Airmail Cover*** – and it was, of course, a matter of pride that you were buying an international airmail envelope from the post office counter... to let the others in the queue know that you had friends in far off lands... the top of the line in Post Office ***'Psho Psha'***... well if Psychology can have a 'P'... why can't Showing Off...?

I gather all this was much cheaper before I was born...

Receiving letters was an equally pristine prerogative in middle class India... and the postman who delivered them – was the much awaited, uncrowned messiah who brought the news of what's happening in the worlds of our near and dear... news – that was good, bad and the ugly...

In a fast nuclear (family) proliferating India of those times, the most dramatic was always the Telegram... the arrival of the Telegram often triggered theatrical trauma... invariably it used to be bad news... ***'grandfather no more – start immediately'***... well – what would that mean – I mean – when did he die? when was this telegram sent? it must have taken at least 1 day for it to get to me? will I reach there by the fourth day? will they be holding on to the body without cremating it? should I go / not go? it takes 2 days by train... and many more...

However, the pleasant news – a wedding or somebody getting a job or my cousin passing her twelfth standard with 60% marks (flying colours - first division)... was always laced with wet turmeric powder on the four corners of the letter... auspicious as it was considered to be...

Graduating to **Archies Cards** – who could say it better than words... and much worse than what I could have said to my Girlfriends, anyway... was quite regressive (literally)... and yet, caused many a crater in my pockets (financially)... the inevitable evil of growing up in teens...

But, buy whatever I did from Archies, the New Year cards were always from the pavements on Janpath and KG Marg (Curzon Road – for those born before me)...

Aw... those Teen Years in Delhi...!

Lucky did not send any cards that winter... neither to his ***Mamaji*** (his maternal uncle), nor to Mamaji's neighbourhood... but I sent Simmy a lot of Cards... the New Year 1992 card to start with... bought from Janpath... then the Valentine's Day card... and the Holi Greetings... and Baisakhi... and a few cards in between with subtle hints around – hey – we could be a couple together...

I got a return card too... in July 1992... her Wedding Invitation... scheduled for later that November... in Jalandhar... no wet turmeric on the corners though... but an auspicious occasion without doubt...

I did not attend her wedding... that was one of the first things Lucky and I did NOT do together...

'Rafeeqi' nibhaayi hai, toh 'Raqeebi' bhi sahi (if I could be a good friend to Lucky, might as well be a good ex-paramour to Simmy)... well...

I never asked Lucky... but he did tell me a few years ago... Simmy runs a flourishing business in haute couture from one of the geographically extended states of Punjab – Ontario – on the east side of Canedda...

19

The Pajero Turns 5...

"We are off the block now... don't tell anybody – it's not out in the press yet, but we have been bought... the board has approved the Sale..."

My Boss had announced – December 2010...

"Boss – tell everyone... just acquired a piece of Real Estate – 12 by 5... 4 wheels... plastic and steel... I 'stopped Press' last night to announce this... my wife has approved it... post facto..."

I had told my Boss – December 2010...

5 years ago, 2 esteemed citizens of this country acquired 2 assets – both spelt P...

In a David - Goliath experiment, Phaneesh Murthy (iGate) with deep pockets, acquired Patni Computers...

And Ravi Kodukula with pockets with many holes, brought the Pajero home...

https://en.wikipedia.org/wiki/Mitsubishi_Pajero

Both Phaneesh and I were asked to leave the firm later... but for different reasons...

"So, who is going to drive the Pajero now?" asked my Mother-in-Law...

June 2014 – my MIL, Smee (my wife) and I were returning from an absolutely un-needed retail therapy – just 3 years and a half after the mighty Leopardus Pajeros - the Spanish Pampas Cat came home...

It was just 2 weeks after the family and I had got back from our summer trip to the US of A...

Landing up on the west side, I had taken to the American roads with a vengeance... from my cousin's home in the Bay Area in Cupertino... to Las Vegas... to the Grand Canyon... to Phoenix... to San Diego... to Los Angeles... and back into Cupertino...

Being an SUV freak for the last few years... and because of my footloose and fancy-free look on my face and a shoestring budget sewn large on my shallow pockets... I had thought of a Ford or a Chevy to rent... and had blocked one almost three months in advance...

Upon checking in at Hertz at their Santa Clara location to pick up the **Chevy Tahoe**, I discovered that was at another location waiting for me with open doors... but if I like, and if I had this impatient, twitchy urge - which I had... I could have a sedan instead...

A brand new aroma and a quintessential mid-sized American sedan...I took the wheel of the **Chrysler 300** when it had just done 273 miles... and had stepped on the gas for the next 10 days...

...and 2,500 miles of rubber kissing the road!

Having not had enough of the road in the west... the New York City - Niagara Falls - New Jersey and back to JFK... was in a **Toyota Forerunner**... that came under my ample backside when it had just come into the JFK Hertz parking... the dashboard read 13 miles...!

Over the next 3 days and another 1,500 miles, I treated the beast... the way the beast deserved to be treated... before I parked it back at the JFK...

Done with the bliss and grandeur of automatic transmission... and landing up back in **'Aamchi Mumbai'** and getting behind the wheel in the Pajero... felt like I had gone back in time...

"Smee – just feel this wheel and the cabin here"... I had taken my wife into the **Mercedes Benz ML350** at Shaman Mercedes at Vashi... the very next Sunday morning after we had come back from Uncle Sam's land...

Every time I hint to my wife the next level of elevation in life, she whimpers... not because she doesn't think we cannot afford the ELEVATION... but she fears the LEVITATION might just cause us hurt when we fall down back on mother earth... **THUD!**

With a scornful look on her sullen face she diplomatically scooped me out of Shaman... before Shaman could make the next move... she had suspected the obvious... she had seen me enough in the last many years of married bliss... that many of my extravagances start with a small little overture... of an introduction to what may be coming our way... okay... my way...

I have this uncanny knack of low spending... I spend once now and then on something I really like and will use on a daily basis – like – say – a car... whereas Smee has this supernatural compulsion for regular spending... like – say – clothes and stones and wardrobes... precious real estate all, you might say...

2 weeks, and many test drives of all the 3 German biggies later... I signed on the **BMW X3** at Infinity Cars, Navi Mumbai...

Only, naturally, the Pajero fell under the hammer and was agreed for a trade in... and the Bimmer would cost me a million (rupees) less if I did that... the contract was sealed... almost...

... till the moment, my MIL happened out of thin air – auspiciously, unannounced and as ordained by a planetary drift...

And that evening... June 2014...

"I am going to trade the Pajero in, for our new car..." I said...

"How can you sell a car that is not even 4 years...?" she almost thundered...

The old world philosopher in her, would not approve of it... anything once bought in her world, should ideally be buried along with you when you die... or given away in charity to those who would not need it any more than you do...

I am dreading of all those silk sarees and jewellery that my wife is slotted to inherit after her... how many more wardrobes will I have to buy... real-estately speaking...

"But, who would drive it, if I don't trade it in...?" I asked quizzically with a wink at my wife... she was already

seething with intrigue for the last few days over this entire proposition of a new car acquisition...

"Why? Why not Meetu?"... my MIL calls my wife, Meetu...

I looked at my wife... and at the Pajero... and my wife back again... there is a definite mismatch... a profile mismatch... but, of course, there was a profile mismatch when I bought the Pajero myself... a Corporate Executive driving a Pajero? – I remembered, my wife had asked me...

"Why not – Smee, will you... er... won't you?"...

That evening – both my MIL and I had virtually tyrannised my wife into driving the Bully... the Leopardus Pajeros – the Pampas cat...

As much as animal lovers feel elated when saving a distraught animal... I felt a high in saving the Pajero that evening... and continue to be on a high each time I gun the Pajero when on long drives...

Meanwhile... Patni Computers continues to exist, in another skin... as Capgemini...

And the Pajero lives on... with Smee and I...

20

A Walk in the Wind...

2 hours, fidgeting inside the cabin as the aircraft is stalled at the far apron away from the main terminal... an extremely engaging 2 hours of a panoramic survey of people's facial articulation... of a faecial expression (read 'crappy')... of a job left less done... or not done... before boarding the flight...

And then when the flight finally takes off... the elation and relief on people's faces and their bowels... the silent prayers answered... prayers, quiet, muffled through a great effort and energy... so as not to sound pompous of having savoured a *"Great Indian Masala Meal"* the previous night...

And now that the flight finally takes off... the silent prayers acquire amplification... distinctly drowned in the din of the aircraft engines... and the white noise in the cabin...

Early morning flights do this to you... **just NOSE UP and FLY...!**

"Ladies and Gentlemen... this is Manisha Gautam, your captain from the flight deck. It's my pleasure to welcome you on board Flight 9W 818 to Delhi... sorry about the delay in taking off late from Bengaluru this morning... conditions way beyond our control... we don't normally see this kind of fog often in Bengaluru, but it is one of those days..."

A very sweet voice from inside the cockpit... almost broke my half dozing neck... when I woke straight up, upon hearing it...

A few flights and about 10 years ago... when women had yet started occupying the seat in the cockpit...

"Ab toh gaye, Ravi Ji... pata nahin yeh auraton ko kyon le lete hain... ab pata nahin yeh aurat hamein sahi utaar paayegi ke nahin..." (We are gone now... a woman flying us... don't know if she will be able to land us safe)...

My next seat neighbour Rajinder Chaudhry had started squirming in his seat right from the time he

108

got into it... this was yet another early morning flight that I was taking to go back home in Delhi...

A midlife staged and an oversized man... who would ideally fit into a seat and a half or more when measured horizontally... and a ceiling and a half, longitudinally... Chaudhry had started complaining about everything under the sun and the ceiling right from the word go... he had got to the airport late by bullying the traffic at Marathalli... got into the check-in counter late... pushed half the passengers out of their wits... bludgeoned the queue at the Security Check and almost got arrested... and finally was the last to board the airplane...

Just to discover that the aircraft was to spend a few more indefinite hours on the tarmac...

Tau... or nearly at the threshold of Tau-dom... Chaudhry struck an instant liking for me despite his puffing and fuming at the eco-system around him... of which, I was an integral part... of which, were the two young women who manned the rear of the cabin and... of which, was Manisha Gautam... who surfaced with the mid flight mandatory pontification that captains and first officers have to deliver every flight...

Striking a conversation with co-passengers comes quite naturally to me... and on that particular morning, I had gone through an ordeal finding myself an aisle seat... and as such, was at loggerheads with the same eco-system of which Chaudhry was a part....

We had settled down at the rear of the aircraft... both Chaudhry and I were lucky... there was no middle seat occupant...

I discovered Chaudhry is a businessman with varied interests in supply chain in the commercial Real Estate... and the Indian Silicon City, with its IT boom, was a key destination on his business map...

"Apna Praaptee (Property) ka kaam hai, Ravi Ji" (I am into Real Estate), he said... and continued to give me Gyaan in his chosen life-space... I had dozed off mid way...

But Manisha's voice over the cabin communication system brought both of us back into the cabin there...

Chaudhry's unconscious bias played out rather unconscientiously... *"Haryane mein toh hum aurat ko choolhe chakki pe chhod dete hain... yeh hawai jahaaz udaana toh hum aadmiyon ka kaam hai, Ravi Ji* (in Haryana, we leave women to home and hearth... flying these airplanes is a man's job)...

I reminded him of **Kalpana Chawla... a Karnal born Indian American,** who flew... a spacecraft...

Chaudhry consciously ignored her... he went on to rant and rave about his 3 sons who are at the brink of worthiness to take on his Real "State" (Estate) binness (business)... what with 2 of them driving Ford Endeavors and the third driving a "sakarpio" (Mahindra Scorpio)... through the length and breadth of Gudgavaan (Gurgaon)... and Niyoda (NOIDA)...

That morning, Chaudhry caused quite a clatter...

And this morning... 10 years later...

Manish Ahuja, brought me back in time...

"Anyway, we took off the moment the fog allowed us... in a westerly direction and turned right towards Mumbai... we are currently cruising at an altitude of 36,000 ft... the outside temperature is minus 49 degrees... but for your comfort, we have maintained a temperature of 22 degrees inside the cabin... the tail wind speed is 8 knots... will help us get faster into Mumbai..." boomed Manish Ahuja, the first officer of my flight from Bengaluru to Mumbai...

Fortunately, Manish is a man... doing a real time manly job... flying airplanes... and Chaudhry was not around with me...

I played out the weather statistics in my mind...

With the commotion of the commode kind... some audibly clear and causing less of air pollution... but many inaudibly causing the silent smells... the quality of the air in the cabin despite the comfortable 22 degrees... was fast becoming a suspect...

I frightfully considered my chances of a Walk in the Wind... with 8 knots... minus 49 degrees...

Chaudhry... it was much safer with you around... your noise pollution was far tolerable than this air contamination... trust me...

Mumbai was very pleasant when I landed up after a 2 hour flight delay... the air smelt fresh, better than the one inside the cabin... a breeze was blowing... a wind was in the making...

A Walk in the Wind... I did...

RECEPTION

21

What They Don't Tell When They Sell...

"Either I am gross dumb or this key doesn't work"... I
told Ali, the smart dude...

I had just checked into the Marriott Hotel and
Convention Centre at Hyderabad this Wednesday...
had lugged my bags to my room on the far corner
of the 6th floor... inserted the key into the slot... and
shock of a surprise!

The door wouldn't just budge open.

Raise your hand if you have lived in a different era...
when the analog locksmiths made those fabulous

locks that would fit into and onto most doors and it was a pleasure turning keys into them and here the clickety-click before the latch opened the door...

Raise your hand if you have been a Bong (Bengali) Peeping Tom (popularly called 'Key Holo') and have used key holes for your elementary sex education...

Raise your hand if you were ever stuck outside your home... or your girlfriend's for that matter, and ever opened the lock – well – by breaking it... So much for a romantic evening – if your girlfriend had a love-hate relationship with her parents... she loved them... they hated me... and every other boy in the neighbourhood...

Not that I was exactly the 'boy-next-door' prototype... but it always pays to rescue a hapless lass by breaking doors open... and pay for the consequences... I was branded the lock breaker of the block and parents started installing digital locks in the neighbourhood...

Back at the Marriott... I stared at the innocuous looking digital lock on my door in dismay... the house-phone on the floor landed me with someone on the other end who said – in a Hyderabadi Accent – *"Hosepeeking (short for Housekeeping)... Can I yelp you"?*

I wondered what kind of hoses this person kept... and she was indeed short of yelping...

When I told her the story... she asked me to go back to the reception and get another key... well... so much for service!

In another hotel, in another era, they used to send someone up with another key... Thank Schindler for small mercies... at least this hotel had elevators...

I lugged my bags back all the way down to the reception... Ali – the smart dude – who had spent 8 minutes and 43 seconds checking me in... looked at the key card that I showed him and realised what he had done...

"Sir – I am sorry – that's the Marriott Loyalty Card... Here is your key card...", said Ali sheepishly...

Ali had spent 6 minutes and 27 seconds of my check-in time selling me the entire paraphernalia of what the Marriott world has to offer... including the complimentary breakfast and the bathtub that comes free with the room... the swimming pool minus Pam Anderson... the spa and massage centre that comes equipped with exotic herbal massage oils imported from Kerala... and a full page of digital (internet) and social (the beer and the bar) network opportunities... at a mere extra cost of Rs 2000 a night and finally the Loyalty Card itself... which he handed over to me...

When he did that, he had said, *"here's your card Sir. Your room no is 6044. Have a nice stay"*...

For someone with limited native intelligence as I... and who was desperately looking for that elusive bed at 9.00pm after waking up at 3.30am in the morning... all cards looked the same exact little pieces of plastic that when fit into some slot or the other... allow you access to – what they should – ideally! Would I give a hotel room key card to the shoe-shop guy while buying those shoes? Hell – no...!

But Ali gave me the Marriott Loyalty card to open my room... #6044. Not a number less, not a number more...

Ali, the smart dude... sold me everything that I did not want... He had also taken a good visual stock of me and purposefully did not mention the Gym... he did not offer it complimentary to me... he knew I would consume the treadmill if he did...

I reflected on everything that they sell you in life... but won't tell you the exact little thing that you wanted to know... my wife's parents conned me into my long-time-and-still-going-swell marriage to my wife and told me about all the nice little things about her... what they didn't tell me is that she DOES NOT snore...!

For the kind of a music buff that I am... snoring is an essential part of my sleep time... I make music when I snore... the clefs, the quavers and the visual octaves that I draw up while snoring would leave Beethoven swivelling in his grave...

And what did we make after we got married? A couple of babies... of course, we make music too... I make the demi and the double flat tones... she makes the demi and the double sharps... honest... OK – just the other way around...!

My parents sold me this life... they didn't tell me I have to work to live... and ever since I have wanted to put some fat into my body... I had to contend to work – rather work it out...

My boss sold me this job in Mumbai... he never told me that my salary will not fit the bracket which could fetch me a few square feet of a *jhuggi* (space in a slum cluster) accommodation on the Altamount Road... next to Mukesh Ambani's Antilia...

Ali - the smart dude - smiled at me when I came back down the elevator again on Day 2... the key would not just work again...

"Did you keep the key card close to your mobile phone Sir? It gets deactivated..." Ali offered the explanation... they say the digital world is binary... it either opens the locks – or it does not...

I checked out of the Marriott on Friday morning... Ali was beaming... I don't know if it was at the prospect of being rid of me...

"Sir – I see that we have two things in common", he said.

Someone is really wanting to strike a rapport, I thought...

"Both of us are Hotel Management qualified and both of us have the same blood group" offered Ali... a philosophical end to this theatrical trauma...

We laughed out loud.

"BLOODY Hell – Be Positive"!

Despite the Loyalty Cards and the key cards and all other things that the Marriott world sold me... Ali, the smart dude... sold me something else that he did not tell me...

Come what may – B+...

Thank You, Ali...

—⁓∽◦◦◦◦◦◦◦⁓—

22

Refer Me Red

"Need a favor, Ravi... I am upgrading my profile on LinkedIn... need for you to give me a great reference in your flowery language..."

Mathuresh (Matt)... had called this morning... exactly 15 years than when we last spoke to each other...

Obviously on both occasions, there was a purpose... the last time, it was him bidding me farewell from one of my previous corporate lives... and this time, it was with a request for referering him on Linkedin...

And did I forget to mention we are connected on LinkedIn... the digital concourse that has helped all the cousins in my 3 worlds, personal, professional

and the 3rd world... just over 7,000 of them... connect
with me ever since we have never met at all... at the
"Kumbh Mela"

Kumbh Mela - best described as the virtual whirlpool
with millions of misplaced microchips... auto-installed
in unvigilant whippersnappers... when they walk
sucked into it... as they come circum-ambulating
to collide with another zillion whippersnappers in a
massed out maelstrom... that can, at its best stretch...
maul in just about 2.4752 million molecules...

*Don't trust me...? ask Wiki... my girlfriend from
Hawaii...*

Matt sounded sheepish... yet confident to make
this demand of me with a straight face... not that I
remembered how exactly he looked then, when we
parted... because in those days all Voice and Accent
(VnA)* trainers in the Outsourcing space looked
pretty out-spaced... or rather spaced out, if you will...
what with a chip on their shoulder, a Martian slouch
and a Venetian gait... they would give you a run-
down look which would place you precisely where
you belong – among mortals...

But hearing Matt's voice on the phone after 15
long years brought back many mushy memories...
well – no – don't get me wrong... my thoughts went
to Vandana (Vandy) – one of the most gorgeous
VnA trainers I had ever met... before I make them

120

VnA trainers sound like a cult by themselves... I remembered Matt was dating Vandy... that was after he was bored of Petra (Pooja)... and before Vandy moved on to Sam (Sameer)...

So much for Call Centre pseudonyms...

"So, you really believe in this LinkedIn reference crap, Matt...? my reference on your profile is going to get you that job that you are looking for...?" I asked Matt after we were done locating the chrono-spatial coordinates of Vandy, Petra, Sam, Neil, Mike, Mandy, Ron and all other team mates that Matt claimed were a part of my team...my extended team that I managed for precisely 3 months and 13 days...

"Well – your designation and your grey hair in your profile photograph are certainly going to have those executive search folks sit right up and take notice of me when they look at your reference comment, Ravi...", Matt prevailed upon me in a childlike way.

While he pumped my ego up, I went into LinkedIn and checked out Matt's profile... I don't know about my profile photograph... but Matt definitely needed to go to a professional photo studio with some decent clothes on... and replace the current photo-shot of his with a new one... one that the executive search folks would die for... more than my reference for him...

"But you know Matt, we had never worked together and I hardly knew you then and even now to write anything about you", I tried to be politically correct.

I wanted to ask him if he knew... if Vandy wanted my reference comment too... I would write anything as long as she asked me... even just once...!

"But that's not really necessary for you to write a comment, Ravi. Do you think all the comments that people carry on their profiles are born out of closely working with or knowing each other? Look at the references that you have already written for people, Ravi. And also the ones that people have written for you. How much of that language is really true for them? You got them there because you love them" reasoned Matt...

This once, Matt hit me where it pricked... he walked that thin line knowing well that this may make me really not write him his reference that he was looking for... I looked at the 12 comments that I wrote for people and the 5 people have written for me... I looked at all the 543 messages in my In Box... which have been waiting for the last many months for the want of some hard hearted honesty... I had consciously not written back to them...

Somewhere down in my heart I knew that there is a Matt out there who would surface someday to be my man in the mirror...! my thoughts went back to all those well-wishers in my life who have always felt good for me... encouraged me... motivated me with kind words... gave me opportunities... hugged me when I was feeling high... lifted me when I was on a low... I may not have known them all well enough... but they showered me a small little gesture when I needed it... They showed that they loved me...

Matt signed off with *"Ravi – color me good. Refer me Red"*

While I write Matt's reference and the others' that have been waiting in the wings...

23

It's a Training Issue...

"Your flight is delayed by an hour Sir..." said Shweta...

"I know that Shweta..." I said... *"I got an SMS and a Voice Response call just 20 minutes ago, while I was halfway through to the airport..."*

My tone had a grudge and a deep degree of sarcasm in it... I looked quizzically at Shweta, with one of my brows raised... what I did not say... which I wanted her to guess, was... *"Hey see, I don't live on the tarmac of the Indian airports nor have I subscribed for the zoo-zoo alerts by the minute. And if your SMS comes in after I have started for the Airport, it isn't of any use to me. I have to reach the airport, spread my feet in the general 'junta' lounge because the other airlines will not allow me into their lounges if I am flying you...!"*

Shweta seemed to have read me... *"But, Sir, I just came in onto my shift. I also came to know of the flight delay only now"* said Shweta with a straight face...

Dressed in a smart, crisp spicy cinnamon red... Shweta was my check in representative at one of the newest low-cost airlines counter that got their license last month... and, of course, she did look like someone who just strolled on to the afternoon shift... because everything about her outer demeanor seemed to suggest that she is all set for another day of the Great Indian Airline Passenger Trauma... passengers, who would, irrespective of the stupid responses that they would get... still always invariably ask the stupid question... why the hell is my flight late...?

To the educated and the frequent flier ears... the response is always a repeat of what Modhumita told you at the IndiGo at Kolkata... or what a Chamundeswari told you in Chennai at the Jetlite counter...

Morning after morning, week after week, year after year, the Great Indian Frequent Flier in me is now tuned to... *"We apologize for the delay because of traffic blah blah blah... the previous flight blah blah blah... and a nut from my wing fell blah blah blah blah blah... a dog on the runway blig blah... fog blah blah... runway in Gurgaon blah... airport in Delhi blah blah... beyond our control blah blah blah and blah..."*

Very recently, I heard the pilot announce the delay was because... *"everything is just about great... all paperwork finished... we are about to take off... but we are stalled on this tarmac because of financial reasons... there are 17 passengers from the Jaipur Jet Airways flight into Mumbai... and they have to go with us to Bengaluru... that aircraft is coming in and landing next to us in the next 20 minutes... as soon as we have boarded those passengers and their baggae... we will be airborne..."*!

Wow – so much for transparency...!

But with Shweta, I heard a completely different take... one that of sheer indifference... which gave her away on where she was on the Great Indian Flight Delay matrix... I knew it was clearly a Training issue...

Well – you would say for a hammer-smith, the entire world looks like one big nail...

And when I heard Shweta... I knew clearly that she was given the wrong script for the day... and since the spicey red counters weren't particularly busy that afternoon... I thought I would want to have a conversation with Shweta...

I asked her... *"What do you think is the least time that takes for someone in this city to get to the airport...?"*

I half expected her to say – our customers normally live on the tarmac or hide themselves inside the pillars and walls of the Departures terminal... built

by GVK, GMR, NTR, MGR, YUR or UBR, and normally
make it in less than a minute...

"Half an hour in the least, Sir," Shweta was honest...

*"So, what use is it if you are to send me the SMS while I
am already driving to the Airport...?"* I asked her...

She was used to this banter by an array of customers
with black hair... brown hair... grey hair... no hair... or
white hair like me... her reply surprised me though...

*"But, Sir, I just came into my shift. I also came to know
of the flight delay only now"* said Shweta.

I burst out laughing – a trifle too loud... for the
comfort of other passengers in some of the other
queues around... and a lot too loud for Shweta's
comfort... I laughed because I could see a reflection
in Shweta – in probably how I used to respond to
customers' questions a few years ago... when I used
to serve credit card and travel customers... The
response was funny in every sense as it detached
Shweta from her employer...

In one master stroke, Shweta told me... do not hold
me responsible for the sagging infrastructure of the
country's airports... for the potholes or the dogs
on the runways or the tarmacs... for the number
of airplanes that have sprouted without adequate
number of runways to support their landings or
takeoffs... or if the runway has been constructed in

Gurgaon and the aircraft has to come to Delhi in the next half hour to dock...

Or rather simply, closer home... if my employer has not got its left hand - right hand act well to inform you in time to make adjustments in your life... to reach and not squat at the airport as your chrono-spatial comfort would allow... or if my employer has not had the financial muscle to build its own real estate at the GVK, GMR, NTR, MGR, YUR or UBR airports in the shape of a private lounge for you to squat... which Mr. Customer, you do not realize... comes at a cost which is slyly built into your ticket price... or if the private lounge is so dear to you and your dear backside to squat out... and if you are so worried about your backside... why don't you go book yourself on a not-so-low-cost-airliner...!

Well, so much for flying low cost airlines – with their not so low cost tag at all...

While Shweta recovered from the cinnamon redness on her face... I said "one day... one fine day... we will all work together to put the Great Indian Flier on to the aircraft on time, every time..."!

Till then... I would leave all our airlines... red or otherwise... contour their training processes to get their representatives to mouth more customer friendly (politically appropriate) replies... scripted or otherwise...

24

The Colour of Death... and SocMed Activism...

My friends Rohit... and Rubina... and Faisal... and Sonal... and Irfan... and all others whose names I have changed here to protect their sanity...

Lest the blue, white and red of the French tricolour that waves on their Facebook DPs is 'temporarily' misappropriated for their allegiance to support the developed world... and as such, could make them possible targets of cyber terrorism...

E.g. - you could be **e-Bombed** if you are a **Facebook** fan... or **i-Bombed** if you are a fan of the Forbidden Fruit... okay – **Apple** for starters...

My friends had changed their Facebook DPs once before recently... when a certain Hoodie-wearing CEO hoodwinked another Barrel-chested CEO into believing that he (the Hoodie-wearing) straight from under the hoodie, supports the 'Digital Revolution' *(sic)*... that he (the Barrel-chested) wanted to bring about in his country... full of wannabes who are bereft of embracing the seed and the fruit of internet... Internet.org... or otherwise...

Over the last week since the Paris killings... because of which we knew of another similar incident a day before Paris... in Beirut... and that the Russian passenger liner 2 weeks before that was downed by the same outfit that claimed responsibility for all 3... or Baghdad... or Damascus... or Nairobi... or Kabul... where the business of terror is 24/7...

I have been wondering, what would prompt a Rohit, Rubina, Faisal, Sonal, Irfan and thousands of other SocMed (read Social Media) activists to "TRY" filter their Facebook DPs...

My good friends and their embracing the country colours... I would love to think... has nothing to do with their preference for a particular flag and its tint or tone... but more to do with how they have transmogrified over the years... from On-Field Activism... to Near-Field Activism... to Coffee Table Activism... to Armchair Activism... to 'Top-of-the-Pot' Activism...

Trust me... the last one is fast gaining currency... activism through your digital interface with the rest of the world... from the top of your pot... in your own space... and at your own time... and by your (own) active thumb... and on your own smartphone...

Consider this...

I live in a '**self trumpeted high-end sarkari cosmopolitan condominium complex**'... this is called the NRI (*Na Rehnewale Indians*) Complex... I am barely home...

Self-trumpted – because it's only us residents who gloat over the haughty high ended-ness and supposedly skyrocketing psf (per square foot) priced complex... despite the all pervasive annihilation of real estate stock in the rest of the country...

And '**sarkari**' – because CIDCO (City and Industrial Development Corporation of Maharashtra... Limited) has built it...

And '**cosmopolitan**' because we have a Kodukula, a Karekar, a Kapoor and a Khan, all connected with each other on Facebook... and all with 'Dil Punjabi' tattooed loud on our tongues... not kidding... ***Chicken Tikka Masala is the national dish of Facebook...***

And '**condominium**' – because it sounds sexy...

In my complex this one telecom provider has politically... and financially... bullied all other networks and rules the roost in both voice and data connectivity... so, Pawar, my next door neighbour on the left... and Malhotra, my 3-doored, pent-housed, an-entire-elevator-to-himself neighbour on my right... have bullied this tyrant of a telecom provider to put up a booster which provides better and faster access to the world...

And where do they place the booster? Right next to my private bathroom... well... a perfect alibi for my 'Top-of-the-Pot' Activism...

But seriously... back to my SocMed activist friends...

My friends... all these and more... have been symbolising a *'SIXTH ESTATE'* in the growing... confirming solidarity through an SMS sent or through a WhatsApp Group Share or vide a 'Like' on the Facebook on many life impacting manifestations... when we want our Judiciary to be more active... when we like a law to be bettered... when one of us in the larger humanity in the world were to be wronged... when we want our Barrel-chested CEO to stay back more at home and push our Foreign Minister to do exactly what she gets paid to do...

I write today... not to shame my friends who have 'filtered' their DPs with the French tri-colour (I dourly do not have a dispensation to do that)... but I want to reflect on what moves us into this 'sixth estate' citizenship...

Allow me to refer to **Henri Tajfel's Social Identity theory**... we band better when we perceive a common enemy...

While the theory itself is dated, it is incidentally, a very useful tool for marketers and is gaining ground in SocMed activism... what with **Facebook now being the biggest country in the world** (more citizens than China!)...

The questions that may interest my friends who filtered the French flag on their Facebook are...

If this indeed makes the world flat...?

Are the SocMed activists outside of the developed world, truly Tier 1 citizens...?

What are the colours of a Lebanese flag? Of an Iraqi or a Syrian or a Kenyan or an Afghani flag...?

When we evidence virtual solidarity, do we see these events as a motivation to control and craft our public persona...? An opportunity to present ourselves as 'good people' and people who are knowledgeable...? **(Psychology of Self Presentational Needs)**

And... more importantly... what is the colour of death? Is it defined by Facebook's 'conditional access flag filtering scheme'...?

25

The Slap Supremacy...

The vain seldom die... so doesn't, the bonfire of the vanities...

The Khan-troversial bonfire seems to be smouldering dead... till **Dangal** stokes it back again next December...

https://en.wikipedia.org/wiki/Dangal_(film)

A year - that's a short time - the pacifist in you would say...

Still shorter - a gullible memory that we carry - I would argue...

But then again, for this ember from the smouldering fire, that flew right into my eye two weeks ago... from Ludhiana in Punjab... that pricks the conscientious commentator in me... the sole custodian of the *Sixth Estate* in this vast psycho-semantic electronic jungle...

Well, this **IS NOT** about Khan... nor **IS** this about the Ludhiana local leader of a free spirited political outfit from the west of the country where I live... who announced a lakh of rupees to anyone who slaps the Khan...

But this IS about the 'Slap' itself...

I have often had this experiential grounding in the way violence is portrayed between two human individuals... in a sharply differentiated manner in the two movie making worlds... Hollywood in Uncle Sam's land and my own Bollywood back home here...

Just imagine... Daniel Craig slapping Christopher Waltz in "Spectre" as a tangible sign of revenge because he was put through 9 precious screenplay minutes of 3rd degree torture... or Aunt May slapping Peter Parker because she would not approve of him wearing that fancy dress Spiderman costume every day to college... especially when she would like for

135

him to be discernibly 'manly' when dating Mary Jane Watson...

And where the physical contest of power is normally through a punch... what the hell... every punch receives a counter punch and it is a long winding saga of violence... till such time either party is tired... or the art of punching itself runs out of innovation...

In Hollyland... everybody is on an equal footing... how socioculturally devastating can that be... psst... *imaginez, s'il vous plait...*

Contrast that with the **'Thappad Theory'** our brothers in Bollywood have put into gross guiltless play over the years... where individual scars and deep levels of despondency are oftentimes settled with a **'thappad'** (the Slap)... a 'slap is duly registered' as a birthright of the 'slapper' to show the 'slappee' his / her rightful place... **'aukaat'** (stature), where s/he belongs...

The father slaps the son... the husband slaps his wife... the mother-in-law slaps her daughter-in-law... the villain slaps the hero (before the hero eventually avenges in the last scene of the movie)... the heroine slaps the hero (before she falls for him towards the middle of the movie)... the master slaps the servant... the elder brother slaps the younger brother... the rich slap the poor... the police slap the wrong-doer...

The slap saga continues...

From – *'mujhe tumhara ye thappad hamesha yaad rahega'*... (I will always remember your slap till eternity)... because one fine day, I will gain a superior social stature to return and give it back to you...

To – *'is thappad ko yaad rakhna... phir kisi akeli ladki ko mat chhedna'*... (remember this slap... never again do you dare to harass a girl when she is alone)... because slap harassment is not about the slap itself... it's about power... and my slap would remind you of where you belong...

To – the super emotive **Sonakshi Sinha** quip – *'thappad se dar nahin lagta sahib... pyaar se lagta hai'*... well, plain interpreted, I am fine with the slap, but don't you dare love me so much...

The slap in Bollywood... and therefore... in the macrocosmic India that I know... is by and large, one of the pivotal manifestations of how the social hierarchy operates in the country... it's a corrective lesson and is aimed less at the body or the face... and more at the soul... and at the sense of who we are... that by the act of slapping, the slapper clearly establishes the line of command and control... the order of supremacy...

The punch however... as much as it is borrowed from Hollywood... and accompanied by aural ingredients like – *'dishum'* and an *'aaee-bushum'* in the older Hindi movies and more recently with the most advanced row and racket of electronic humdrum of the punch... often invites that inevitable last sequence in the movie... of the hero bashing the villain in an 'all is well that ends well' storyline...

And would you remember the last time when a slap in Bollyland provoked a 'slap back'?...

Naah... the logic of reverse slapping does not fancy the figment of our filmmakers' fascination...

And the sound of the slap?...

Well, it just sounds as it should... **SLAP**...

But there is always this sooth-saying (sic) in this double slap... weigh this up... the 2 slaps... Slap... and Slap... the left and the right cheeks for balance of power... the supreme end of the script and screenplay...

'Aaj main tumhe tumhara thappad sooth sameth lauta raha hoon'... I am returning your slap with compound interest – a benign act of accomplished revenge... this 3 hour movie itself would have been rendered redundant without this recall and response... today I have gained that social stature which puts me above you... and therefore... this aural illustration... ***Fattaaaekk***...

I remember when I was a kid just about stepping into my teens... for a fault indescribable even in an easy erasable electronic space as this... my father had slapped me hard...

That had hurt... physically... in the 3rd degree... as a child...

Today... I can rationalise... in the *Sixth Estate*... as an adult...

But that day, it just did not matter who was right... that day, many years ago, the slap demonstrated where I belonged... in the social hierarchy... the father, the elder, the major and the physically mightier... may always have the right to rightfully place the rest of the world in the right hierarchy...

In Ludhiana... 2 weeks ago... what did the slap supremacy convey?

Let no Answer be Unquestioned...

26

Curtains… and the Connecting Room…

Innovation in the air… not in my Macbook Air… but in the hotels that you step and sleep in…

Except the Minibar… the Bathtub… the Pillows that you sleep on… the Curtains… and the Connecting Room…

Stepping into the many hotels that I do… with the whir of the proximity card that you touch on the circular little pad that indicates green when the code matches in the elevator… and on the circular little pad on the door of your room… comforting you that the receptionist has given you the right card for the right floor and the right room...

It is a great feel...!

After all, after a weary 12 hour flight – home to hotel – you would not want to start up grappling with a key that does not let you slump on your bed...

And then the Moments of Truth...!!

The curtains make you struggle the first... the ease with which the ring looped curtains used to open in the past... you now find 'oversimplified electrically motor driven one sheet for the entire 12 feet window' curtains... controlled from another 'oversimplified and remotely placed electronic panel', next to your bed... the switches – with an 'up' and a 'down' arrow pointed indicators – are a part of this electronic panel... with just about 35 and a half other controls to toy with...

You check in when the sun was up... by the time you figured the curtains on the electronic panel to get a view of the outer world... the sun is out and set... Welcome to the next world...

Stepping into the many hotels that I have done... the next thing that hasn't changed in many years... is how you start searching for the Minibar... since it is always low and below the TV mantelpiece this one isn't bad...

except, lifting up one leg in the air to maintain your centre of gravity... ensuring your spine is north-south in parallel polarity to mother earth... ridding your mind of sins that you are picking that Coke up (Diet Coke these days)... ssshhhluk... you pull the trigger on the can and... glug... glug goes in the Coke...

... Why the hell have hotels not innovated to get the Minibar to the eye level... or say, the hand level... like the microwave in my kitchen at home... why do I have to stoop low and die of guilt to pick that can up... why do I have to bend and bow in reverence to the Minibar... what if, with my raised leg, I feel the urge to do what dogs do with raised legs...

And all the effort for a can of Coke...?

In so far about 100 and above hotels that I have stayed in... there isn't one single bathroom that looks like the previous one... particularly the umpteen knobs that turn to get the water flowing... left... no... right... hot water please... the water starts pouring from the tap... it's cold... and wet... now, which is that knob that switches the water from the tap below to the shower above... and a third to the hand shower...

And blessed you are, if you land up in a bathroom with a multipurpose bath area – the shower inside the bathtub... and with no rubber mat below your feet to protect your standing up to the shower... hang on to the shower curtain for your dear life...

And in other bathrooms... the water does not flow with the turn of one knob... you have to synchronise with nano-precision, another button that turns along with the first knob... the last bathroom had a similar soft panel in the bathroom, as in the bedroom with another 15 and a half electronically jutting soft touch buttons...

Welcome to the touch baths... iBath... anyone...?

I would think the bed is the most innovated, to date... and the simplest to figure out... 20 years ago, when on my first business trip, I checked into **Holiday Inn at Kowloon, Hong Kong,** it had a mattress, a bed sheet, a blanket and a bed cover... today with all the innovation... my bed at all hotels ever since has – a mattress, a bed sheet, a blanket and a bed cover...

Guess what... The bed in my most recent hotel in Manila gave me a choice of 4 types of pillows to sleep on... **Soft – cotton**; **Ultra-soft** with Ostrich feathers; **Semi-hard** – they did not mention the animal or the bird or its body parts – but in fine print there was a hint towards one found extinct in the Tundra region; and finally **Hard** – well this one completely skipped any insinuation towards any vegetation living or dead...

Now... I am a simple man... but, with a quiet, experimenting deportment... would try anything once in life... the first night I mounted the Hard pillow... had the Semi-hard to support my supple spine...

straddled the Ostrich between my legs and had the
Cotton to comfort my skull...

Well... somewhere towards the end of the hour, the
Ostrich started squawking... the Tundra softened up
because of being out of the Arctic for long... the Hard
pillow mount was more discomforting than a pair of
ill-fitting underpants... and the only thing that still
held its promise was the Cotton...

So much for Pillow Prosperity...!

Finally, something has to be done about the
Connecting Rooms... whosoever thought a man pays
for all the luxuries of a life in an upmarket hotel and
still wants to be with clangour and clash for company
through the night... has to think twice... or have the
rooms sound proofed...

Or the least – the hotel needs to tell the occupants
in conjoined rooms that they need to be discreet
when they step out of their rooms in the morning...
one man and two gorgeous looking women stepping
out for breakfast in the most impressionable
early morning fashion-wear is NOT appropriate,
appreciated and acceptable to the guy next door –
i.e., I... what after all that clink, clank, clunk, clatter of
the night...

The biggest respite are the TV channels... none
of them make sense... for somebody who sparsely
watches TV, hotel rooms with a TV screen on the wall,
are the most divine reminder of how self restrained

life can be... of how you can read more books than stare endlessly at the screen in front of you...

Till I discover the eccentricities of another life... in another hotel...

27

Empathy, Sympathy… and Dharampathy…

Every morning, I wake up to the thud in my macrocosmic mind… the illusory image of a **7 billion** human faces looms large in front of a yet blurry eyes that are half woke…

The optical illusion zooms in to the **70 thousand** people that I pass by while on my way to work and back… another **7 thousand** that may glance at me as I zip past them or halt my car at traffic lights… where my personal practice over the years has usually been to look to my left (I live in the fast lane – drive in the right lane where available)… that momentary glimpse and a customary nod with a smile to my fellow driver parked next to me… and the smile in return, connects me to that part of humanity that I see in my left lane...

With a whir, the camera in my mind closes up to those **700** odd faces that I work with or meet in my cafeteria for my lunch or that sundry snack every day... and to the 70 people on my work-floor, some of whom I meet in the washrooms...

And those **7** precious people that I really breathe my life in and out with... my wife... my two children... my live in domestic help (she is my wife's lifeline – and, so, infallibly mine)... my parents (with whom I remote breathe my life - a lifeline about 350km from where I live)... and I...

The one final look before I step out of the house... at the microcosmic I... **the Man in the Mirror**... and I stop short of whispering within my voice chords...

Is that the sperm that finally won?

Empathy... believe me... manifests in myriad ways...

"I heard about your Boss... my sympathies with you..."

11 years ago, I had recently got promoted and was moving roles... and cities too... and I was moving to this Boss who was one of my internal customers and a very dear one at that... who chose to take me along

while he himself was moving roles... brands... and cities...

The least that you would expect from friends who love you and your upward mobility... and friends up, close and personal, is... *"Congratulations – you won a lottery... fare well"*...

After all, a life without friends is like death without witnesses...

But here was **Prashant**... one of my very good friends and peers from a previous life... and who incidentally had this future Boss of mine as his Boss until then... and for the very obvious calamitous phenomenon unfurling in the cosmos at that time... my promotion and my precious moment of pride and glory... could not have gotten more condoling than that...

I thought it sounded like... *"I heard about your Loss... my wholehearted condolences..."*

I was hurt... maybe not as much as jumping on a bicycle without a seat... but it still hurt...

I guess, both of us... Prashant and I... were pubbing a little too heavy on fuel and fire in the last few weeks leading up to my promotion... and Prashant's mild-boros as the preferred nicotine for breakfast wasn't helping either... I did not realize it at that time but having grown in the firm together, Prashant and I were almost like brothers in arms... and he, having suffered our common Boss until then, the common sufferings were proving to be stronger bonds than common joys...

Common sufferings... as they say... knit hearts closer together... and succumbing to the phenomenon – we all love to hate our Bosses... is universal... and more common the Boss, the stronger the compassion...

SYMPATHY... however is not more demonstrable than some of the other heartwarming events that fold out in my life...

Like this one...

"Ravi Sir"...

A strident voice... from one corner of the corridor in a glitzy, semi-done mall in Gurgaon... about 8 years ago... when I myself, was an upcoming star in my chosen professional space of giving Gyaan and Gospel... serving sermons, both pleasant and the unpalatable... and getting away with it unscathed, demi-bruised, organic and kicking...

What with such desirable consequences as... when this voice comes closer... accompanied by a full body, twinkling eyes in one of the most zestful faces that I have ever met in my life...

Shalini bends with reverence running down her spine... and almost touches my feet till I pull off in embarrassment... and with an unmatched, out-of-breath energy in her voice, says... *"Ravi Sir... remember me... you taught me how to give and receive feedback, a couple of years ago, when I joined the company... that was worthwhile... I use it in my life even today..."*

No... I don't remember Shalini... at least not until she re-introduced herself that day... I have this unburdening megalophobia... I cannot remember people's names when I meet them after 9 hours of separation from my Training Rooms... well - that's probably the way I am gifted...

I had just started sporting white hair at that time... and this small little pigtail with a blue rubber band... and it felt like... ***GURU-DOM*** had finally kicked in...

And when that happens, ***BABA-DOM*** isn't far away...

That sets in complimentary, 'state-of-arrival-in-life' emotions... ***EMPATHY*** for the entire humanity... or at least, the part of the 7 billion that I would touch through my Baba-dom... and ***SYMPATHY*** for people like Shalini... my trainee in my professional life who truly believes she can give feedback to people and they would do something about it... and for Smee... my wife in my personal life who truly believes she can give ME feedback and I will do something about it...

Well... my Baba-dom may not bother Shalini... until I diversify from my Gyaan and Gospel world and come back with the launch some of my ayurvedic wellness products and find some retail shelf space...

But my renunciation of the material world will definitely help Smee (my dear wife) alleviate some pain from life... after all... as her **DHARMPATHY** (her husband – ME), I have enjoyed every moment of staying married to her... it's so great to find that one special someone that you could annoy for the rest of your life...

The thought of Smee... my dear wife of 18 years now... and the zoom out to the 7 people... and the 70... the 700... the 7 thousand... the 70 thousand... and the 7 billion...

I feel so connected to the Universe...

And to the Man in the Mirror...

―⌇∿∘⌀☉⌀☉⌀☉∿∘⌇∿―

C.R.A.P

Cold... Rolled... Annealed... and Pickled...

Thank You... for dealing with this CRAP...

Author Bio

Ravi Kodukula
scribbles random
thoughts around
riddling events in life
between work, drive,
drink, eat and sleep
for many years...

With a following of 13 non-flinching fans... two of
them being his children who are his ardent critics, Ravi
got confident about taking his scribblings to press...

Ravi likes keeping life simple and tries finding various
hues and shades of humor in life's non-descript
situations... at times likes to push the humor to
satire...

Like many in his generation, Ravi has lived various
lives... has been a cook and waiter; an ad space
salesman; a call centre representative; a travel agent;
an avid traveller amongst others...

Ravi lives in Navi Mumbai with 1 wife and 2 children...

Ravi can be reached at: 2016crap@gmail.com.

Printed in the United States
By Bookmasters